Approaches to Poetics

Selected Papers from the English Institute

APPROACHES
to
POETICS

Edited with a Foreword by Seymour Chatman

Columbia University Press   *New York & London*   1973

Acknowledgment is made to M. B. Yeats and Macmillan of London
& Basingstoke, and the Macmillan Company of Canada, for permission to quote four lines from "The Coming of Wisdom with Time,"
from *Collected Poems* of W. B. Yeats; to Macmillan Publishing Co.,
Inc., for permission to quote four lines from "The Coming of Wisdom with Time," from *Collected Poems* of W. B. Yeats (copyright
1912 by Macmillan Publishing Co., Inc., renewed 1940 by Bertha
Georgie Yeats); to The Society of Authors, on behalf of the Bernard
Shaw Estate, for permission to quote an extract from *Major Barbara*,
by George Bernard Shaw; and to First Casualty Press, for permission to quote the poem "S.O.P." by Larry Rottmann, reprinted from
Winning Hearts and Minds: War Poems by Vietnam Veterans (all
rights reserved by 1st Casualty Press, 1972, P.O. Box 518, Coventry,
Connecticut 06238).

Library of Congress Cataloging in Publication Data

English Institute.
   Approaches to poetics.

   Papers delivered at the annual English Institute,
held Sept. 2–5, 1972.
    1. Literature—History and criticism—Theory, etc.—
Congresses. I. Chatman, Seymour Benjamin, 1928–
II. Title.
PN441.E53   801'9   73-8969
ISBN 0-231-03781-3

Foreword

STRUCTURALISM, as M. Tzvetan Todorov points out,
is an ideological trend in the social sciences—
linguistics and anthropology in particular. It is an intellectual
movement, comparable to other -isms—like Neo-humanism,
or Freudianism. It is not a field of inquiry but an approach to
inquiry, one approach among others. So whether or not the
contributors to the 1971 and 1972 English Institute sessions on
linguistics and literary study—or those whom they explicate
—are in fact structuralists (or antistructuralists) is less important than the nature of the field engaged. The answer, it seems
to me, is not literary criticism but "theory of literature" or
"poetics" (in the sense in which Todorov uses the term *poétique*).
Poetics in turn, as it is popular in Europe to maintain, is a branch
of semiology, the general science of signs and sign systems
(where "sign" is used in the technical sense of the fundamental
unit in the interchange between parties in the communicative
act). Despite the strangeness of the term to American ears,
semiology was largely the invention of an American philoso-

pher, Charles S. Peirce, and was developed by his disciple Charles Morris. In Europe today it is a broadly studied field; there are important centers of semiology in Paris, Milan, Tartu, Amsterdam, Copenhagen, Budapest, Warsaw, Urbino, Konstanz. Journals are currently appearing with titles like *Semiotica*, *Poetics*, *Poétique*, and *Journal of Literary Semantics*, and excellent introductions to the subject have been written by Pierre Guiraud (*La Sémiotique*), Georges Mounin (*Introduction à la sémilogie*), Luis Prieto (*Messages et segnaux*), and Umberto Eco (*La Struttura Assente*).

Are literary features—like plot, like meter, like point of view—in fact semiological structures? (I take it that nobody would deny that they are at least structures; even high school textbooks of literature have constant recourse to the term.) As Professor Hugh M. Davidson points out, a structuralist like Roland Barthes would argue that a poem or novel is not "primarily an art-object or an act of knowing or feeling. It is significant language, signs used in a special way." But what exactly does this mean? To be semiological, a structure must be in some sense meaning-bearing in its own right. Now obviously literary structures "bear" meaning insofar as they present their content: Milton's blank verse epic (that names two of the structures of the manifold) "bears" an account of the fall of man ("account" names a third structure, that of narrative). The question, however, is: Is "epic"—the empty form —an independently meaning-bearing concept? It depends on what you mean by "mean." It is hard to imagine a literary scholar seriously arguing that "epic" is empty of all independent significance, although the nature of that significance is clearly other than that which actual sentences in English or any language refer to. Regardless of how residual (or connotative or whatever) such significative elements may be, or how difficult they have been to grasp, they are clearly *there* in some important sense.

Literary structures are not to be identified simply with their linguistic manifestation. To say that everything in literature comes to us finally through words is to say nothing very profound. It is increasingly clear that linguistics per se can tell us little about important literary structures. Plots clearly exist in narratives that are not communicated by means of words —in a mime by Marcel Marceau, a ballet, a cartoon without dialogue bubbles, a Chaplin film. Indeed, it might be said that a central problem for poetics is to distinguish more clearly the nonlinguistic from the linguistic structures in literature and to show how the former are communicated, both at deep and at surface levels. This is not a question of interpreting texts in the usual literary-critical sense, but rather of determining how structural information is acquired by the reader (i.e., what semiological mechanisms are entailed). How, for instance, do we come to sense the covert presence of a narrator even in a third-person "limited point of view" novel, though the word "I" is never used?

A word about the arrangement of these papers. The first three are on the key Formalist and Structuralist theorists— Roman Jakobson and Roland Barthes. Professor Victor Erlich's paper continues the authoritative account of Jakobson's work begun in his book *Russian Formalism*. English scholars will welcome an opportunity to examine Jakobson's method as applied to a familiar text.

Professor Hugh M. Davidson's paper is an explication of certain of Roland Barthes's ideas, and Professor Frank Kermode's is a critique of one of them, the distinction between closed and pluralistic texts. They should be read in that order by those who do not have previous knowledge of Barthes's work.

Professor Davidson surveys Barthes's critical presuppositions in general, as illustrated in *Critique et vérité*, and then examines his practical criticism in terms of the more recent *S/Z*, Barthes's microscopic analysis ("microanalysis") of the structural levels of Balzac's story *Sarrasine*. Professor Kermode challenges Barthes's distinction between the classical narrative text, characterized by a limited or "parsimonious" plurality of sense, and the "ideal" (elsewhere the "modernist") text, of infinite plurality, possessing a veritable "galaxy of signifiers," not a structure of signifieds (see p. 54 below). He claims that even in such relatively staid texts as Henry Green's *Loving* there is no simple closure, and the situation is still more complicated in more modernist work, like Anthony Burgess's *MF* and Thomas Pynchon's *The Crying of Lot 49*. There is, finally, no such thing as parsimoniously plural (or *lisible*) texts: all texts prove to be infinite in some way (*scriptible*). Not, of course, that Professor Kermode would go back to the academic, historically relativistic criticism attacked in *Critique et vérité*: ". . . we can have," he urges, "a humanly adequate measure of plurality without abandoning all notions of structure" (p. 78). In other words, no particular analytical mechanism is needed, for "the novel itself has long been aware of its chimerical potential."

Professor Richard Ohmann's paper further develops ideas

on the relevance to literature of John Austin's Speech Act theory, ideas offered in several earlier essays (see below, footnote 25, p. 136). This theory, he maintains, is especially useful in accounting for the dynamic aspects of literature. His examples are mostly from drama, where the illocutions are especially clear. Whereas structuralists concern themselves with questions of *lisibilité* and *scriptibilité*, the Speech Act theorist's *mot-clef* is "felicity," the relative well-formedness of utterances at the illocutionary level (as compared to grammatical well-formedness at the locutionary level). His explication of "infelicitous" passages from Samuel Beckett seems particularly illuminating. Venturing into the ontology of literature, Professr Ohmann finds the Speech Act theory a good way of demonstrating that a text is not the simple sum of its words and syntax. It permits him a new approach to the ancient concept of mimesis, both in terms of author ("The writer puts out imitation speech acts *as if* they were being performed by someone," p. 98) and in terms of a reader (who decodes by "build[ing] on his tacit knowledge of the conventions—past and present, actual and possible—for illocutionary acts" p. 99).

Professor Stanley E. Fish's paper is a broad critique of a range of scholarship usually called, more or less roughly, "stylistics." Among examplars, he questions the purely quantitative approach (Milic), generative stylistics (Ohmann, Thorne), and recent British (Neo-Firthian) efforts (Halliday). Professor Fish argues that none of these takes proper account of the reading process itself. The result is "banks of data that are unattached to anything but their own formal categories" (p. 131). In language reminiscent of Barthes's, Professor Fish urges that the reader be conceived as giving meaning to a text rather than extracting it. Even stylisticians who have tried to account for the reader, like Michael Riffaterre, manage somehow to discount his most vital functions. Professor Fish calls for a new kind of stylistics—"affective stylistics"—to bring the reader into the theoretical picture in a more genuine way. Critical of previous utilizations of Speech Act theory (Ohmann), his own formulation is based on John Searle's version of that theory.

The contribution of M. Tzvetan Todorov is at once the most general and the most programmatic of the group, and for that reason I have given it the last word. M. Todorov dares to ask for a science of literature, but even as he waves the red cape, it is clear that "science" is not being used in a sense that any good Aristotelian could seriously object to. In terms not unlike those of René Wellek and Austin Warren, he asks that literature be approached internally rather than externally, and that literary theory be separated from literary criticism (the description and interpretation of specific texts). Noting that poetics is a millennia-old discipline, M. Todorov asks for a typology of discourses, so that what is peculiar to literary discourse may emerge in clearer contrast. As a possible path into this effort, he reechoes the Russian Formalist idea that global literary structures are in some sense expansions of local devices—that a plot, for instance, may be essentially an "unfolded" metaphor. Hence, he feels, the idea of literary endogenesis is not unfeasible.

University of California, Berkeley   Seymour Chatman
February, 1973

Contents

Approaches to Poetics

VICTOR ERLICH

Roman Jakobson: Grammar of Poetry and Poetry of Grammar

IN A MUCH CITED theoretical paper Roman Jakobson advanced the following thesis: "Textbooks believe in the occurrence of poems devoid of imagery. But actually scarcity in lexical tropes is counterbalanced by gorgeous grammatical tropes and figures. The poetic resources concealed in the morphological and syntactic structure of language, briefly, the poetry of grammar and its literary product, the grammar of poetry, have been seldom known to critics and mostly disregarded by linguists, but skillfully mastered by creative writers." [1]

"The poetry of grammar and the grammar of poetry." This dual formula has been for over three decades now the leitmotif of Jakobson's wide-ranging structural analyses of poetry. Several factors can be held responsible for Jakobson's increasing preoccupation with what one of his favorite English poets, Gerard Manley Hopkins, has called the "figure of grammar." A leading exponent of Formalist-Structuralist poetics, Jakobson had always been sharply critical of the traditional overem-

[1] "Linguistics and Poetics," in *Style in Language*, ed. Thomas A. Sebeok (New York, 1960), p. 375.

phasis on lexical tropes. In the early days of Russian Formalism his spirited challenge to the view of poetry as "thinking in images" was couched in Futurist or, if one will, Dadaist terms. "Poetic speech," argued Jakobson in his pioneering study, *Modern Russian Poetry* (1921), "tends toward its ultimate limit—the phonetic or, more exactly, the euphonic word." [2] Yet before long the fixation on "sheer sound" in the Formalist writings yielded to a broader and more mature notion of poetic discourse whose hallmark, it was now felt, lay not in the absence of meaning but in the multiplicity of meanings. "The aim of poetry," wrote Boris Eikhenbaum, "is to make perceptible the texture of the word in all its aspects." The "actualization" of the verbal sign achieved by poetry was recognized as a complex transaction, involving, in addition to euphony, the semantic nexus inherent in the word, as well as the grammatical patterns discernible within the poem. The late Formalist concept of verse was predicated upon the proposition that no significant dimension of poetic language could be deemed irrelevant either to the over-all effect of the poem or to its local triumphs.

Yet to say that something is potentially relevant is not necessarily to insist that it is likely to be paramount. The special appeal of the "grammar of poetry" to a champion of structural linguistics and poetics rests in large measure on the status of grammar in discourse, poetic or otherwise. To quote an articulate critic of Jakobson, Michael Riffaterre, "Grammar is an actual geometry of language which superimposes abstract rela-

[2] *Noveyskaya russkaya poeziya. Viktor Khlebnikov* (Prague, 1921), p. 68.

tional systems upon the concrete lexical material, hence grammar furnishes the analyst with ready-made structural units." Jakobson himself urges in his most extended statement on the subject—"The Grammar of Poetry and the Poetry of Grammar" (1960)—a "profound analogy between the role of grammar in poetry" and that of geometry in painting.[3]

Another causative element in Jakobson's methodology was the linguistic texture of his initial test-cases. Owing to their strongly inflectional character, Slavic languages have at their disposal a host of morphological devices whereby important distinctions, such as those between direct or indirect object, between a recurrent or a single act, can intelligibly be made. Thus, an affectionate and sophisticated immersion in Slavic poetry, guided by a keen awareness of the poetry of grammar, was bound to bring to light telling instances of an effective poetic utilization of the "potential dramatic force of the Russian morphological categories." [4] This is precisely what happened in the late 1930s when, preparing a Czech edition of Pushkin's selected works, Jakobson had occasion to subject to close scrutiny several "touchstones" of Russian verse. In fact, his dissection of the verbal dynamics of Pushkin's narrative masterpiece, *The Bronze Horseman*, remains to this day one of the most straightforward and persuasive applications of the method under discussion. The poem, in part a powerful re-creation of the 1824 Petersburg flood, dramatizing the vulnerability of the

[3] "Poeziya grammatiki i grammatika poezii," *Poetics. Poetyka. Poetika* (The Hague, 1961), p. 408.
[4] "The Kernel of Comparative Slavic Literature," *Harvard Slavic Studies* (Cambridge, Mass., 1953), I, 15.

city's populace to the elements—a matter scarcely considered in Peter the Great's grand design—is a confrontation
between two ill-matched protagonists. They are Peter the
Great, or rather his bronze statue, a symbol of imperial power
which towers over the city and the defiant Neva, and the
crazed "little man," Evgeny, whose dream of personal happiness has just been washed away by the flood. The narrative
reaches its dramatic peak in Evgeny's tragically ineffectual rebellion, a short-lived challenge to the heartless "idol on a steed
of bronze," followed by a panicky flight. It was Jakobson's
characteristic and original observation that the contrast between Evgeny's helpless frenzy and the Bronze Horseman's
unshakeable might and staying power was conveyed, in part,
by a strategic use of verbal aspects. Every declarative sentence
featuring Peter uses the imperfective aspect which connotes indefinite duration. Conversely, the story of Evgeny's abortive
rebellion moves through a succession of breathless perfectives
which suggests abrupt, disconnected, frantic acts.[5]

If Jakobson's explorations of his favorite Russian master im-
pelled him powerfully toward the grammar-of-poetry and po-
etry-of-grammar formula which was to become his trademark,
the dual concept had not acquired this status until his postwar,
American phase. In "The Kernel of Comparative Slavic Literature" (1953) he posited the wealth of grammatical, and especially morphological, tropes as one of the characteristic though
obviously not unique resources of Slavic poetry. In "Linguistics and Poetics" (1958) he spoke of grammatical figures as an

[5] *Ibid.*, pp. 15–18.

important and hitherto vastly underestimated dimension of poetic craft. Finally, in a programmatic statement read at the Warsaw Conference on Poetics in 1960, he offered a wide-ranging agenda for the structural analysis of the grammar of poetry bolstered by rich illustrative material which, in addition to three Slavic poems (two Pushkin lyrics and a sonnet by the Polish Romantic C. K. Norwid), includes Andrew Marvell's "To His Coy Mistress" and a fragment from Sir Philip Sidney's "Arcadia."

The following decade offered Jakobson several opportunities to test and implement this ambitious program. Moving with characteristic ease from culture to culture, often in collaboration with knowledgeable and occasionally distinguished "native informants," he has probed grammatical configurations in the Russian Symbolist Alexander Blok, in Cavafy, in a Portuguese poem, in two Baudelaire sonnets, "Les Chats" and "Spleen," and most recently in Shakespeare's Sonnet 129. The most famous of these exegeses are "Les Chats de Charles Baudelaire" (1962),[6] written jointly with Claude Lévi-Strauss, and *Shakespeare's Verbal Art in "Th'Expence of Spirit"* (1970),[7] written with Lawrence Jones. I would like to attempt a tentative assessment of Jakobson's methodology in the light of these two salient instances.

Les amoureux fervents et les savants austères
Aiment également, dans leur mûre saison,
Les chats puissants et doux, orgueil de la maison,
Qui comme eux sont frileux et comme eux sedentaires.

[6] *L'Homme*, II, No. 1, 5–21.   [7] The Hague–Paris, 1970.

Amis de la science et de la volupté,
Ils cherchent le silence et l'horreur des ténèbres;
L'Erèbe les eût pris pour ses coursiers funèbres,
S'ils pouvaient au servage incliner leur fierté.

Ils prennent en songeant les nobles attitudes
Des grands sphinx allongés au fond des solitudes,
Qui semblent s'endormir dans un rêve sans fin;

Leurs reins féconds sont pleins d'étincelles magiques,
Et des parcelles d'or, ainsi qu'un sable fin,
Etoilent vaguement leurs prunelles mystiques.

Predictably, the Jakobson–Lévi-Strauss analysis of the above Baudelaire sonnet is intensely preoccupied with syntactic and morphological ingredients. At an early phase of the argument, chief emphasis is laid on what is described in a more recent study as "pervasive features," that is, correlations and frequencies which dominate the sonnet as a whole. A close relationship is postulated "between the hierarchy of rhymes and the choice of grammatical categories." All lines, it is noted, end in either nouns or adjectives; all feminine rhymes rest on plurals. All personal verbal forms and all personal pronouns, as well as all grammatical subjects, are couched in the plural, with the exception of lines 7 and 8 and the central distich. (The significance of this deviation from the poem's norm will be touched upon below.)

The bulk of the meticulous linguistic description of "Les Chats" is geared less to the over-all grammatical cum metrical characteristics of the poem than to the manifold morphological and syntactic parallels or contrasts between its various juxta-posable segments. Dissected along criss-crossing—vertical or horizontal—lines, the poem emerges as a system of systems, an intricate web of binary oppositions.

A painstaking reconstruction of the poem's compositional framework yields a tripartite division into quatrain 1, quatrain 2, and a sestet, and three systems based on the binary principle. These are, respectively, (*a*) the two quatrains vs. two tercets dichotomy, (*b*) the outer vs. the inner strophes, and (*c*) a con-figuration that pits the opening six lines and the closing sestet against the central distich.

What are the salient grammatical and lexical correlatives of these modes of segmentation? First, our attention is drawn to syntactic parallelisms between the octet and the sestet, for ex-ample, the occurrence of relative clauses in both or the preva-lence of animates in the first quatrain and the first tercet and of inanimates in the second quatrain and the second tercet. The chiastic figure which links the opening quatrain with the final tercet features contrasting subject-object relationships. Thus, in the outer strophes, the subject and the direct object belong to the same semantic category (animate in the first quat-rain, inanimate in the second tercet). Not so in the inner units. In the first tercet, an inanimate object (*attitudes*) is pitted against the animate subject (*ils*), while in the second quatrain an identical configuration (*ils*→ *silence*) alternates with the an-imate object–inanimate subject pattern: *l'Erèbe*→ *les*. "Strik-ing grammatical parallels" are observed between the beginning and the end of the poem. Such features as the wealth of adjec-tives (the first line contains only adjectives, two of which, *savants* and *amoureux*, are substantivized), two subjects sharing one predicate, or predicates accompanied by adverbs (*aiment également / étoilent vaguement*) occur only in these portions of the poem.

Yet the most distinctive grammatical profile is assigned to lines 7 and 8: *L'Erèbe les eût pris pour ses coursiers funèbres / S'ils pouvaient au servage incliner leur fierté*. The central distich contains the only proper noun in the poem, the only grammatical subject and predicate couched in the singular, the only conditional mood forms suggesting an "imaginary action" (*eût pris, s'ils pouvaient*), and the only instance of an inanimate subject governing an animate object (*l'Erèbe les eût pris*). The clear implication here is that these blatant departures from the poem's prevalent grammatical hierarchies enact or dramatize the pivotal place of the central distich in the dynamic progression of the poem, in its "thematic" movement.

How do Jakobson and Lévi-Strauss envisage this movement? "The two quatrains present the personality of the cat as seen from the outside, while the two tercets effect its transformation." Each successive strophe provides the cats with a new identity. The opening quatrain relates them to two antithetic realms of experience—the sensual and the intellectual. The cats are allowed to transcend their animality by providing a common ground for, and thus mediating between, ardent lovers and austere scholars. The second quatrain injects a pejorative note as it plays with the possibility of the cats' being reduced to an animal and ominously subservient role of *coursiers funèbres*, only to deny it emphatically in the closing line. (The inherent pride of the cats militates against their enslavement, which is surreptitiously desired by the forces of darkness.) If this briefly suggested and promptly repudiated identity points beyond the poem's "sedentary," domestic, indeed claustrophobic locale, the mythological *Erèbe* leads through the sphinx simile into what Jakobson and Lévi-Strauss call "le miracle des chats," as the house which initially encompasses and circumscribes the cats opens out into a torrid desert. The ontology of the poem undergoes an equally dramatic, indeed a double transformation. First, the image of languid domestic pets gives way to that of sphinxlike creatures who in turn disintegrate, in a series of synecdoches (*leurs reins féconds, prunelles mystiques*), into luminous particles of matter, into sensual electricity. Thus, the movement of the poem, pointed up or undergirded by the grammatical peculiarity of the central distich and the "vertical" contrast between two successive portions of the poem, is from claustrophobia to boundlessness, from cozy darkness to luminosity, from enclosed cats to liberated cats (*chats en liberté*). Moreover, the concluding sestet projects into the cosmic plane the antinomy inherent in the first line of the poem. *Leurs reins féconds* harks back to the *volupté* of the lovers, the *prunelles mystiques* to the vision of the scholar. *Magiques* refers to the erotic glow of the former, *mystiques* to the contemplative attitude of the latter.

The concluding portion of the Jakobson–Lévi-Strauss study urges, somewhat unexpectedly, an implicit equation in Baudelaire's sonnet of cats and women. Some of the evidence adduced is culled from two other Baudelaire poems, both of which bear the title "Le Chat." One of these contains the line *Je vois ma femme en esprit*, the other injects explicitly the theme of sexual ambiguity—*Est-il fée, est-il dieu?* The tendency to blur the boundary between sexes is alleged to be present, though in a more oblique fashion, in the sonnet under discussion, to wit, the androgynous quality of *les grands sphinx* and the "paradoxical choice of feminine nouns as bases for so-called masculine rhymes."

I realize that this sketchy and truncated summary fails to do justice to the intricacy and ingenuity of the Jakobson–Lévi-Strauss analysis. That analysis is, without any doubt, an impressive demonstration of how the keen eye of an imaginative linguist can discern a wealth of "subsidiary patterns" within the verbal tissue of a highly organized utterance. What makes this performance significant and at least partly successful is the authors' determination to link meaningfully at least some of the grammatical tropes detected in the sonnet with its over-all thematic thrust. By bringing out the latent drama of grammar the critics seek—and occasionally manage—to clarify the poem's dramatic structure.

Yet I must own up to residual doubts about the validity of this brilliant exegesis and its broader implications. I will defer the larger issues until the end of this essay and confine myself at this point to strictures bearing specifically on the Jakobson–Lévi-Strauss reading of "Les Chats."

In an interesting article, published in the Structuralism issue of *Yale French Studies*,[8] Michael Riffaterre takes exception to both the methodology and the conclusions of "Les Chats de

[8] "Describing Poetic Structures: Two Approaches to Baudelaire's *Les Chats*," *Yale French Studies*, No. 36–37 (1966), pp. 200–42.

Charles Baudelaire." I find myself in partial disagreement with this polemic: I do not share Riffaterre's apparent assumption about the "irrelevance of grammar," nor am I taken with his concept of the "superreader," who in this particular instance would encompass Baudelaire, Gautier, who paraphrased "Les Chats," Jules Laforgue, who echoed it, as well as the best translators and analysts of the sonnet. Such composite entities are not likely to prove a better guide to the optimal interpretation of the poem than is the text itself. The ideal reader is defined by the inner exigencies of the poem rather than the other way around. Yet certain of Riffaterre's specific cavils have merit, I believe.

According to Riffaterre, some of the "systems of correspondences" posited by Jakobson and Lévi-Strauss fail to "contribute to the poetry of the text." The point is not easily dismissed. Even if one were to discount, or postpone for later consideration, the admittedly tricky problem of the actual availability of these "systems" to the ordinary reader's aesthetic perception, we ought to pay heed to the possibility that some of the partial or total grammatical correspondences between comparable metrical units do not actually work in the context. Thus, as Riffaterre has pointed out, to posit an equation between *Qui comme eux sont frileux* and *Leurs reins féconds sont pleins*, on the basis of syntactic parallelism and internal rhymes, is to disregard important differences between these phrases. The internal rhyme *eux-frileux* is much more "obvious" than *reins-pleins* because a "natural reading of line 12 would have to take into account the tight unity of 'leurs reins féconds' which demands a pause after 'féconds' and because

'pleins' cannot be severed from 'd'étincelles magiques.' " Moreover, the homologous relationship between *comme eux sont frileux* and the following phrase *comme eux sedentaires*, more
immediately compelling than the correspondence between
lines 4 and 12, tends to preempt the latter in the reader's actual
perception. To put it more broadly, it stands to reason that
some parallelisms brought to light by linguistic analysis may
fail to be "literarily active" because they are too incomplete or
too remote and thus liable to be superseded by more proxi-
mate, "obvious" relationships.

Riffaterre's strictures about the alleged significance of the
high frequency of the plurals in "Les Chats" also deserve attention. The fact itself is not at issue. Yet the proliferation of the
plurals often appears here to be strongly suggested by the nature of the subject, rather than by the poet's choice—
conscious or half-conscious. The poem is not about a cat, but
about cats. Such notions as "pupils" or "loins" appear naturally
in pairs. Finally, such nouns as *ténèbres* are used only in plural.

The core of Riffaterre's article calls into question the
interpretation summed up above and offers, at length, a different reading. My own feelings are mixed. The Jakobson
analysis does a remarkable job, I feel, of piloting the reader
through a carefully reconstructed grammatical cum phonetic
and lexical maze, from the domestic emphasis of the opening
quatrain through the sphinx simile to the "magical" and
"mystical" glitter of the closing lines. Yet it is at least arguable
that the authors' partiality to binary oppositions, for example,
anterior vs. posterior, has led them to overstate such transformation as is taking place here, to overdramatize the contrast

between the beginning and the end of the poem. In Riffaterre's view, which I largely share, there is much in the portrayal of the cats (*puissant, orgueil*) that foreshadows both the *nobles attitudes / Des grands sphinx* and the final apotheosis. To put it differently, what Jakobson and Lévi-Strauss call the "miracle of cats" is prefigured and qualified in the paradox of cats and cat lovers. Within the context of the first strophe, the *amoureux fervents* and *savants austères* are not simply antipodes whose only common ground is shared affection for cats. The terms of reference are partly interchangeable. The ardor of the scholar's intellectual quest and the "austere" single-mindedness of the lovers, totally preoccupied with themselves and each other, converge on the image of a sedentary hankering for the ultimate in knowledge or emotion. This paradox or inner tension is not resolved but magnified into the sphinxlike image of "immobile mystic concentration." By the same token, the finale implies not so much a "removal of boundaries," as a bounded mystery, a grounded transcendence. The cats' affinity for *le silence et l'horreur des ténèbres*, asserted in the second quatrain, is not entirely repudiated by the magical sparks issuing from the cats' loins or by the mystical glow of their pupils. "Magic" is not unrelated to darkness (e.g., *black* magic); "mystique" suggests esotericity—dark, secret knowledge—as well as illumination. Rather than celebrating a straightforward triumph of light over darkness, the imagery of the final tercet suggests the theme of light-in-darkness. Not a wholly unexpected ending, one may add, for a poem launched by such paradoxical notions as passive quest, gentle power, and fussy (*frileux*) grace.

Yet, since a significant shift of emphasis and a gradual widening of perspective does occur in the course of the poem's argument, one might remonstrate that the core of the Jakobson–Lévi-Strauss interpretation is a dramatic overstatement of an essentially valid insight rather than a misreading. Less credit is due to what Riffaterre calls the "afterthought" of the two critics, notably their suggestion about the implicit parallel between cats and women. Granted that the sphinx simile "pushes" cats toward an androgynous state. Granted, too, that the electricity of their *reins féconds* can be easily interpreted as indeterminate, generalized sexuality. Yet the grounds on which the cats' female or bisexual nature is posited are methodologically precarious. Not only is the crucial lexical evidence extraneous. In addition, and more important, the "paradoxical choice of feminine nouns as a basis for masculine rhymes" is not germane to the problem of the cats' sexuality. One does not have to be a professional linguist to realize that, while there is no point-to-point correspondence between masculine gender and male sex, the former category is actively involved with the sex boundary. Not so "masculine rhyme"—which is simply a "faded" prosodic metaphor. Clearly, one of the risks of applying linguistic concepts to poetry lies in the analyst's occasional tendency to "reify" his terminology, to mistake a metalinguistic fiction for a poetic reality.

Th'expence of spirit in a waste of shame
Is lust in action; and till action, lust
Is perjur'd, murd'rous, bloody, full of blame,
Savage, extreme, rude, cruel, not to trust:
Enjoy'd no sooner but despised straight;
Past reason hunted, and no sooner had,

Past reason hated, as a swallow'd bait
On purpose laid to make the taker mad:
Mad in pursuit and in possession so;
Had, having, and in quest to have, extreme;
A bliss in proof, and prov'd, a very woe;
Before, a joy propos'd; behind, a dream.
All this the world well knows; yet none knows well
To shun the heaven that leads men to this hell.

Shakespeare's Verbal Art in "Th'Expence of Spirit" brings
Jakobson's dual formula to bear on a poem whose status in the
Shakespeare canon has been widely contested. If J. C. Barber
hailed Sonnet 129 as one of the greatest poems in the language,
John Crowe Ransom denied it "any logical organization" and
J. M. Robertson found some of its lines so weak and anticli-
mactic as to warrant skepticism about Shakespeare's author-
ship. As Jakobson and Jones embark on their inquiry into the
"subsidiary patterns of a phonetic, syntactic and semantic nature" (Charles Rosen) that undergird the poem, they clearly
proceed on the assumption that "Th'expence of spirit in a
waste of shame" is an eloquent testimony to the Bard's consummate "structuring" skill which Ransom's iconoclastic essay
capriciously calls into question.

In this momentous sortie into Shakespeare's scholarship, Jakobson's *modus operandi* is essentially the same as it was in
dealing with "Les Chats," though his more recent argument is,
perhaps, somewhat easier to follow. The presentation is lucid
and crisp, the underlying terms of reference succinctly spelled
out. Once again a metrical description is followed by a careful
reconstruction of the poem's "compositional framework,"
through the medium of such dichotomies as odd against even,

outer against inner, anterior against posterior, the terminal
couplet against the quatrains, and the center against marginals.
The entire analytical sequence is preceded by an eminently
sensible provisional interpretation or, as the authors put it,
"tentative explanatory rewording" of the sonnet. A pithy semantic exegesis is offered toward the end of chapter 9, "Couplet
against Quatrains."

Viewed *in toto*, we are told, the sonnet exhibits "a con-
spicuous alliteration or repetition of sound sequences and
entire morphemes or words" (e.g., "ex*p*ence of *sp*irit,"
"*bl*ouddy/*bl*ame," "*m*ake/*m*ad," "proof/proved"), high inci-
dence of infinitive forms in even lines, and an absence of "personal or corresponding possessive pronouns." Rather surprisingly, one may note in passing, the authors have failed to draw
from this latter observation a thematic inference which is made
explicit by Charles Rosen, in one of the more thoughtful
assessments of *Shakespeare's Verbal Art:* "Sonnet 129 written
on the most personal of themes—fornication and its bitter
aftermath . . . is not only 'generalizing' but absolutely, even
repressively, impersonal."

Yet the main energies of the study are concentrated in the
chapters which bring out the intricate segmentation of the
poem. Charles Rosen finds chapter 6, "Odd against Even," the
most disappointing. I do not quite agree, in part because the
section contains what Rosen himself calls a "brilliant exemplifi-
cation of the poetry of grammar," notably the observation that
"both animates of the sonnet, the two which pertain to the
personal (human) gender, function as direct objects in the last
line of the even strophes—*taker* in 'on purpose layd/ to

make the taker mad,' *men* in 'to shun the heaven that leads men to this hell.' " This, Jakobson and Jones correctly argue, is a striking departure from the "common usage where the unmarked agent of the verb is an animate . . . and the unmarked goal is an inanimate." "In both cited constructions with transitive verbs the sonnet inverts this nuclear order. Both personal nouns characterize human beings as passive goals of extrinsic, non-human and inhuman forces." Here is a proposition which is not only intrinsically valid but also clearly relevant, since it relates tangibly the grammatical patterning of the even strophes to what the authors recognize elsewhere as the central theme of the sonnet, the motif of the "tragic predestination," the notion of man as a helpless victim of his sexual appetites.

According to Jakobson and Jones, the odd vs. even dichotomy has yet another implication. The contrast between the proliferation of modifiers—adjectives and participles—in the odd strophes, and their virtual absence in the even ones, is said to point up a significant difference of thematic emphasis. The even strophes which feature antithetical shifts in the luster's attitude from desire to self-disgust "center upon the process of metamorphosis"; the odd strophes present the "different stages of lust *in abstracto*," introduce a "retrospective and generalizing approach." Again a sound and, possibly, important point. Yet I agree with Rosen that the force of observations such as these is not enhanced by the conscientious listing in the remainder of the "Odd against Even" chapter of relatively minor binary correspondences or noncorrelations, for example, "the preposition *in* appears only in the odd strophes."

The next phase of the argument pits the first quatrain and the terminal couplet against the second and third quatrains. Here much emphasis is laid on the "higher syntactic rank" of the outer strophes, notably a greater frequency of finite forms, for example, *is, knowes, leads*. Conversely, the inner strophes are characterized by intricate echoing effects: "a word which terminates one line . . . is repeated at the beginning of the next line"; the same root keeps recurring, each time in company of a different affix (*injoyed/joy, had/having, proof/proved*). While descriptively these statements are unassailable, it occurs to me that the "higher syntactic rank" of the outer strophes might be a somewhat less distinctive feature than the lexical "redoubling" or morphological interlacing discerned in the inner units. The authors themselves tend to concede that much when they assert that the former contingency is observable in "many four-strophe poems in world literature." Perhaps the point could be generalized. Might we not assume that the first and the last movements of the poem, which respectively introduce the theme and seek to resolve it, are more likely to tend toward formal propositions and thus toward finite forms than do the intermediate segments?

Though the anterior vs. posterior dichotomy is dutifully invoked, it seems that the previous two are more strategic as foci of grammatical contrasts and correlations. "Within each of the two contiguous strophic pairs . . . grammatical contrasts between neighboring strophes play an incomparably wider role than specific similarities in their grammatical structure." This might be the reason why such relationship as obtains between the first and the last two strophes is stated in "thematic" rather than grammatical terms: "the first, outer odd strophe towering above the subsequent even strophe heralds the immutably murderous essence of lust, whereas the terminal, outer even strophe imposes upon the posterior strophic pair the concluding, strenuous theme of the inescapable, infernal end." An acute observation, to be sure, but one which is susceptible to a less "binary" formulation. The movement from a full-throated denunciation of lust to the quietly held out prospect of damnation is, as Charles Rosen points out, subtly modulated from strophe to strophe. Moreover, it could be argued that, in a sense, the first strophe towers not only over the subsequent one but over the entire poem. The fury of the initial verbal onslaught reverberates through the sonnet and gradually subsides, without ever yielding, some of the critics notwithstanding, to a different, more positive view of lust.

This brings us to the next phase of the analysis and the problem of the relative status and grammatical structure of the terminal couplet. The two concluding lines, which embody a generalization of the poem's theme and state its underlying tension—bliss vs. woe—in religious terms, are, on any reading, a crucial segment of the poem. Predictably, the authors find them grammatically distinctive as well. The terminal couplet is said to be lacking in parts of speech which proliferate in the three quatrains—adjectives, participles, indefinite articles—while containing the only plural substantive in the poem (*men*) and, as already mentioned, a relatively large number of finite forms. The terminal couplet, it is further asserted, "opposes concrete and primary nouns to the abstract and/or deverbative nouns of the quatrains." I am

not entirely happy about the above, since, especially in the
context, neither "heaven" nor "hell" can be properly described
as concrete nouns. But the succinct statement of the poem's
two interlocking themes occasioned by these juxtapositions
strikes me as cogent. It deserves to be quoted at length:

> The sonnet has two topics—the lust and the luster—and
> omits the designation of the former in the final strophe and
> the designation of the latter in the initial strophe. The ab-
> stract appellation of the first topic attracts a string of further
> abstract nouns. The first strophe characterizes lust in
> itself; the second launches a set of passive participles with
> a hint to yet unnamed dramatis personae and finishes by re-
> ferring to the *taker* of the *bayt;* the third strophe uses active
> participles to depict the taker's behavior and bring forward
> images of lust as objects of his strivings. The adjective *ex-*
> *treame* applied to lust in the first strophe is transferred to the
> luster in the third. Mere anaphoric pronouns refer in the ter-
> minal couplet to the previous representation of lust and the
> notion of the luster grows into a generalized idea of men
> and their damnation. The final line seems to allude to the ul-
> timate persona, the celestial condemner of mankind.[9]

I am tempted to conclude my hasty summary on this con-
structive and lucid note. But the standard Jakobson analysis
cannot run its course without invoking yet another dichotomy, that of "center against the marginals." Once again the assumption about the pivotal role of the central distich is but-
tressed by references to the grammatical differentia of lines 7

[9] *Shakespeare's Verbal Art in "Th'Expence of Spirit"* (The
Hague–Paris, 1970), p. 27.

and 8 which include the absence of such pervasive features of the marginal lines as parallelism. At the same time the central lines contain "the only simile and thereby the only syntactic instance of a comparative construction 'as.'" As always, the linguistic description is unexceptionable, but one wonders how useful or rewarding is the juxtaposition in the context under discussion. It is true that, taken as a separate unit, lines 7 and 8 differ in their grammatic proclivities from the preceding as well as subsequent lines. But how legitimate, let alone imperative, is such a separation here? Obviously one of the salient contributions which line 7—"Past reason hated, as a swallowed bayt"—makes to the patterning of the poem lies in echoing, with a significant variation, "Past reason hunted" of line 6. Under such circumstances, how central is the concept of a central distich?

In spite of occasional misgivings or quibbles, I find it difficult not to agree with I. A. Richards that *Shakespeare's Verbal Art* is "very likely to prove a landmark." More broadly, Jakobson's two most famous inquiries into the grammar of poetry contribute significantly to our understanding of how poetic language actually works. By interlacing skillfully various strands in the verbal tissue of the poem—the phonic, the grammatical, and the lexical—these analyses press vigorously beyond the obvious and easily discernible toward the "subliminal structure" of the poem (I. A. Richards). The attempt to bring to light configurations and strategies of which not only the "ordinary reader" but often the poet himself is not likely to be aware is admittedly fraught with serious risks. Not the least of them is the danger of mistaking the critic's mental set for the intent of the poem. Yet a quest for "subliminal" structures should not be abandoned prematurely. I. A. Richards's distinction, made in his admiring account of the Jakobson and Jones monograph, between the poet's "knowing about" and "knowing how" may well be heeded.

When so much intellectual energy and enthusiasm, so much acumen and "spirit" is expended in the service of a laudable goal, it may seem ungenerous and picayune to indulge in cavils or caveats. Yet my demurrers are not meant to detract from the impressiveness of Jakobson's performance. They are testimony, rather, to the immense difficulty of the task he had set himself and to some inherent limitations in the linguistic approach to poetry, or, for that matter, in any method, however rigorous and well-thought-out.

In a recent statement on stylistics and literary scholarship, René Wellek maintains that for all their virtuosity and meticulousness such analyses as "Les Chats de Charles Baudelaire" cannot tell us "anything about the aesthetic value of the poem." A dense sound structure or an intricate grammatical organization per se "does not establish a high poetic quality." I quite agree. But since, ostensibly, inquiries such as those undertaken by Jakobson purport to demonstrate "*how* the poem works" rather than *how well* it works—though at certain levels of analysis the distinction is, admittedly, difficult to maintain—the more urgent query is: how relevant is inquiry into the grammar of poetry to the *interpretation* of the poem? To what extent and in what ways does it further the objective invoked by I. A. Richards, that of helping us "read better"? On this score the admittedly sketchy evidence adduced above is less than conclusive. In both instances firm if intermittent links were forged between the phono-grammatical and the thematic dimensions of the sonnet: significant insights were secured and some arbitrary misreadings avoided. Beyond that, our two test-cases differ appreciably. On balance, in "Les Chats de Charles Baudelaire" the explication of the poem hinges more directly, for both better and worse, on the reconstructed grammatical underpinning than is the case with *Shakespeare's Verbal Art*. For better, since a demonstrable connection between composition and theme tends to validate the analysis. For worse, because, though the core of the interpretation in the Baudelaire paper is largely sound, the authors' methodological bias leads them to overstate the interstrophic contrast at the expense of intrastrophic tension, and because their overinvolvement with linguistic terminology suggests to them a far-fetched "afterthought." On the other hand, the Jakobson reading of Sonnet 129 appears to me unexceptionable and thus clearly superior to wrongheaded surmises alluded to in the concluding section of the monograph. Yet only some elements of this interpretation depend visibly on the formidable linguistic machinery brought into motion presumably in order to substantiate or generate it. There are instances where the analyst's uncannily keen eye for grammatical tropes helps elucidate the text. Thus, having been alerted to the poem's proclivity for syntactic parallelism we will be more likely to read, as Jakobson and Jones correctly recommend that we do, "before, a joy proposed/ behind, a dream" as beforehand a proposed joy, afterwards a phantom. By the same token, as shown above, what Jakobson and Jones called a reversal of the nuclear order in transitive constructions which occur in lines 8 and 14 points up the central motif of man's vulnerability to forces beyond his control. Yet many correlations adumbrated in the monograph, though valid and ingenious per se, are not so demonstrably usable. Therefore, when the authors confidently state that "an objective scrutiny of Shakespeare's language and verbal art . . . reveals a cogent and mandatory unity of its thematic and compositional framework," one is inclined to wonder just how mandatory this unity actually is —or has been shown to be—throughout the Jakobson-Jones exegesis.

Granted that the impressive documentation of multidimensional verbal patterning in Sonnet 129 invalidates J. C. Ransom's assertion that Shakespeare is often "nonchalant" about structure. But do we really need the intensity of Jakobson's concern with "grammatical figures" in order to call into question Ransom's willful denial to "Th' expence of spirit," along with many other Shakespeare sonnets, of "any logical organization," in order to repudiate J. M. Robertson's even more extravagant charge of verbal impotence, or R. Levin's psychologistic view of the poem? To focus for a moment on the last-named, one's skepticism about Levin's reinterpretation of Sonnet 129 as a retrospective account of a hypothetical protagonist's actual sexual encounter and his gradual recovery from bitter disgust that follows in its wake would be vouchsafed by widespread awareness of the "generalizing" quality of the sonnet, an awareness fully shared and cogently articulated by Jakobson and Jones, but certainly not unique to their study.

I want to make my position clear. I stand with Jakobson and

the entire Formalist-Structuralist tradition in assuming the potential relevance of grammar to the explication of the poem. I agree with Boris Eikhenbaum that no dimension of poetic language is immune to the impact of the Poetic Process. Yet the fact that grammar, like any other facet of the poem's verbal structure, can be, and often is, relevant does not mean that every grammatical correlation discerned by the linguist's keen eye is equally "operative" (I. A. Richards).

This brings me to the larger and, possibly, the central issue. In view of the multidimensional quality of the verbal sign, every speech act is an immensely complex transaction. Every extended verbal utterance entails myriad distinctions—phonic, morphological, syntactic—whose comprehensive description would tax the resources and the patience of the best-equipped linguist. This is doubly true of poetry: the tight unity of the verse line intensifies the interaction between individual words and word-sequences. It is an elementary psychological fact that not everything that at closer inspection turns out to occur in the poem can be apprehended by the most alert reader. Yet it is possible to go further and assert that not every element or pattern in the poem which is susceptible to linguistic description is stylistically, poetically, or aesthetically significant.

We have been told repeatedly, and with justice, that poetry is the most highly organized and most teleological mode of discourse. We know—or ought to know by now—that in verse, as distinguished from informative prose, the word is not aesthetically neutral, that it is, or tends to be, an icon rather than a tag or a vehicle. The poet, especially the great poet, often bends language to his own characteristic purposes, including those of which he is only dimly aware, and in the process brings into focus, consciously or otherwise, various organizing principles which inhere in his medium. Yet his power to reshape or dramatize it is hemmed in by what I might call linguistic contingency. Whenever a poet selects a word, his choice, whether made on lexical or on euphonic grounds, is likely to have consequences, often of a grammatical nature, consequences not only unintended by him but, more importantly, not germane to the intent of the poem. "The form must remain overdetermined," says Charles Rosen. If he means that we should not attempt to assign poetic significance to all determinants, I fully agree.

How does one distinguish between the elements of the poem which are operative and those which are not? This, clearly, is one of the most difficult and one of the most important questions that confront a structural analyst of poetry. It stands to reason that the most relevant configurations are those which can be most tangibly related to other dimensions of the poem and, above all, to its essential thrust. The obvious difficulty with this confident answer is that our sense of that thrust is derived in large measure from attending precisely to those "subsidiary patterns" whose poetic relevance is yet to be demonstrated. Are we faced here with a vicious circle? Or is it rather the circle of hermeneutics—"a continuous movement between the whole text and the interior forms"? (Charles Rosen). We infer our approximate sense of the whole from a preliminary yet careful scrutiny of the "interior forms." Armed with this provisional insight, we return to the poem in order to listen to it still more closely, and at length, and in the process to modify and expand our original perspective. Is it too churlish to suggest that when we do so, our choice of cues should be guided less by our over-all methodological commitment than by the distinctive tenor or texture of the work before us?

If, in the end, my predominant response to Roman Jakobson's brand of structural poetics is one of abiding intellectual gratitude, the fact is due in no small measure to the analytic brilliance and the rich literary sensibility which he brings to bear upon his seminal formula. Even as I balk at Jakobson's injunction that linguistics be allowed to "direct the investigation of verbal art in all its compass and extent," [10] I delight in a man whose characteristically generous error lies in equating the competence of his major field with the truly poetic élan of his own scholarly vision.

[10] "Linguistics and Poetics," p. 377.

HUGH M. DAVIDSON
Sign, Sense, and Roland Barthes

IN THE FALL OF 1965 Raymond Picard, a professor at the Sorbonne, and well known for his exhaustive research—basically historical in conception—on Racine, published a short but explosive little book entitled *Nouvelle critique ou nouvelle imposture*.[1] While it is clear that Picard intended to question the procedures of a whole group of new critics in France (Sartre, Poulet, Richard, Mauron, Goldmann, for examples), his principal target was Roland Barthes, director of studies at the Ecole pratique des hautes études, who had published in 1963 a volume of essays on Racine done in one of the new modes. Barthes took as his main point of departure the proposition that Racine's characters form a horde or tribe of about fifty people, dominated by harsh father-figures usually at war with their sons over women and power. Picard was not at all convinced by this mixture of anthropology and psychoanalysis. By the time his rebuttal was finished, he had attacked Barthes for subjectivity, for violating the elementary rules of scientific thought (or, for that matter, of articulate thought), for cynical and obsessive preoccupation with sexuality, for unverifiability, ambiguity, contradictions, aberrant extrapolations, jargon, inaccuracy, incoherence, arbitrariness,

[1] Utrecht, 1965.

ideological impressionism, dogmatic fantasy, ignorance of scholarship, galloping systematization, and so on.

In February of 1966 Barthes gave his riposte, entitled *Critique et vérité*.[2] Some of his compliments, if less luxuriant, were hardly less deadly: Picard, he said, represented the interests of an intellectual caste; he spoke and defended the critical language not even of yesterday but of the day before yesterday; he was attached to fantomatic models of thinking and to a number of tautologies, linguistic myths, and stereotypes; and, as his supreme weakness, he suffered from *asymbolia*, or the inability to understand the symbolic language of literature. But there was light as well as heat in this reply, some of which deserves at least a quick review. After that introduction to the critical position of Barthes, I want to go on, in the second part of this essay, to a discussion of his latest and most remarkable book of criticism, *S/Z*.[3] I believe that *Critique et vérité* and *S/Z* taken together lead us directly into the way of thinking and some of the conclusions that have caused Roland Barthes to be generally recognized as one of the initiators of the science of semiology in France and one of the most original advocates of structuralism as a way of approach to the study of literature.[4]

In the first of these works Barthes evokes on the one hand the hostile camp of university criticism—*la critique*

[2] Paris, 1966.   [3] Paris, 1970.
[4] The first section of this essay reviews briefly the main points made in a longer presentation published in *Criticism: Speculative and Analytical Essays*, ed. L. S. Dembo (Madison, 1968).

universitaire—with Raymond Picard, of course, as one of its most distinguished representatives, and, on the other, a different type of criticism, one that he has described with various adjectives. Perhaps the most satisfactory are contained in the phrases *critique idéologique* and *critique d'interprétation*. He marks off thus a rough grouping, composed of people who, in their discussion of literature, use one of the principal intellectual languages now being spoken, who find their vocabulary and grammar, so to say, in Marxism, psychoanalysis, structuralism, existentialism, or phenomenology. (As a matter of fact, he argues, university criticism is a *critique idéologique* without realizing it; but it just happens to embody the ideology of two or three generations ago.)

Now a particular type of this ideological or interpretative criticism is what interests Barthes. Let us begin by noting that he admires linguistics, especially the structuralist kind. We are not surprised, therefore, to find that the reality he turns to at the start of his own reflection—the logical start, I mean—is *language*. To know literature one must first know language, since the former grows as a sort of parasite-system on the principal system formed by the latter. The truth of this proposition has become quite clear in the last hundred years, he thinks. From Mallarmé to Blanchot, writers have constantly recognized that language is both the matter and the sphere of literature (p. 38).

Once decided upon, this step, this assimilation of literature to language, affects everything else. The literary work is not a thing, or more precisely, language transformed into a kind of object, as it is for some of the Formalists in this country. Nor is it essentially a kind of mental activity, like the aesthetic intu-itions posited by Croce, or more recently, like the tight species of dialectical thinking that fascinates Georges Poulet and that he finds everywhere he looks, or, again, like the concrete workings of sense and imagination that fascinate Jean-Pierre Richard, for whom the literary work is a key to the writer's encounter with the world. I realize that the true state of affairs is quite complex; still I think it obvious that Barthes does not see in the work primarily an art-object or an act of knowing or feeling. It is significant language, signs used in a special way.

"Significant" and "sign" are very important words here. Barthes borrows from Ferdinand de Saussure the distinction of *signifiant-signifié-signe*, the first referring to the vehicle, the second to what is conveyed, and the third to what comes into being through the association of the other two. By a special twist given to the notion of the *signifié*, what is signified, Barthes establishes the specific order of literary language. When language is involved in *praxis*, in activity designed to modify a situation, it is transitive, aimed at something beyond itself, and, indeed, limited in what it signifies by the situation to be changed. The natural tendency of language toward am-biguity is thus checked by the circumstances. But literary lan-guage is *in*transitive; there is no external situation surrounding literary language and restricting its semantic possibilities. As a result, such language becomes *symbolique*, that is, plural, ca-pable of sustaining more than one sense. It is enigmatic, like an oracle, and the critic composes, rather than recovers, the sense of it, with the aid of vital elements present in *his* situation.

Where we are going can be indicated if we return for a moment to Raymond Picard. Picard once said in an interview that Barthes conceives of language as something intermediate between rubber and molasses. He (Picard) believes rather in the notion of a recoverable historical sense for a work and for the language in which it is written. He further conceives of this sense as a function of a period or moment in the history of a civilization. If, after managing this task of recovery and referral—and the effort of self-denial implied in it—the critic wishes to see the relevance of the sense to his own time, he is free to do so. But as far as Barthes is concerned, to give such emphatic attention to the historical and, for him, literal sense is to reveal that asymbolia that I mentioned earlier. No one sense may be set up as a canon. The work is a question or sign that has no answer or sense until a reader or critic furnishes one out of his own history, freedom, and language.

In fact, and it is essential not to miss this further point, Barthes calls upon the critic to *write* something that is consubstantial with what the author wrote. In satisfying this condition the critic must elaborate a sense that respects the symbolic character of the literary language: symbol must seek symbol (p. 73). Thus, as the work was written, so must the critic read and write. The need to harmonize the language of the work and the language of the critic is related to the recent change in the relationship of criticism to literature. Since Mallarmé, the two functions—poetic and critical—of writing have tended toward exchange, interpenetration, solidarity. The metalanguage of criticism accompanies and extends creative activity, so that now there is only one kind of writing (p. 46).

In *Critique et vérité* Barthes replies to one objection that is frequently addressed to him: that his conception of criticism leads fatally to subjectivity in interpretation. He lists three sanctions that apply to criticism as he understands it: (1) It must take everything into account; it must find a place in a system of meanings for every detail. (2) It must proceed according to definite rules; however, these will be derived, not from a model of scientific reasoning in the usual sense, but from the logic (as yet only partly developed and understood) of symbolic language. Here linguistics will be powerfully aided by psychoanalysis, which already can provide some of the formulas by which polyvalent language may be understood— either from the analysis of persons, as practiced by Freud and others, or from the analysis of substances, as exemplified in the works of Gaston Bachelard and his disciples. (3) It must move always in the same direction, assuming the same conditions accepted by the writer, and, in particular, the basic one that *language*, not the *person* speaking (and, as we might say, "expressing himself"), is the subject under consideration. If these three sanctions are observed, the critic is not by any means free to say *n'importe quoi*. Bound by the kind of rigor befitting his inquiry, he will trace out in a work long chains of transformations, developments of themes, and series of images.

The pages in which Barthes develops these points introduce us to some of the most characteristic concerns of the *nouvelle critique* in France. In one place he tells us that the movement is national in character, with little or no debt to Anglo-Saxon criticism, to Spitzerism or to Croceanism. I shall take this remark as the point of departure for a comment or two. During the last thirty-five years the nature and history of literary criticism have been widely explored here and in England. This exploration has made possible some awareness of the types and limits of literary criticism, some discernment of the patterns involved in the frequent changes of alliance and fortune that seem to be its lot, some understanding of the philosophic bases that underlie persistent differences of approach, and some appreciation of the unavoidable irony in it, since what it says in any one instance reminds us constantly of all that is being left unsaid. I think that we can assert, in the light of this experience, that controversy over the legitimacy of the *nouvelle critique*, insofar as it is a coherent, self-conscious, responsible movement, is unnecessary, in this country at least. That being true, we can turn our attention from clashes of principle to the problems of defining and situating it, of studying its results and standards of performance.

One further remark. It is impossible to miss the resemblances between this polemic in France and some of the discussions in American criticism in the period from about 1935 to 1960. There is the taste for immanent (we said "intrinsic") values in literature; there is the hostility to literary history, the tendency to oversimplify and caricature it, with the answering strong reactions from the representatives of that discipline; the decision to ask many of the important questions in terms drawn from linguistics and semantics, with some revival of interest in ancient rhetoric and poetics; the effort to distinguish literary language from other uses of language (American New Critics usually preferred negative analogies with *science*, while Barthes prefers to say that literary language has nothing to do

with *praxis*); the inclination to turn to the inventors of techniques for exploring pre- or extralogical forms of thought (we
had Frazer, Freud, and Jung; Barthes has Lévi-Strauss, Lacan,
and Bachelard).

Well then, in 1966 Barthes thought of himself as a member
of a group of new critics and in some degree as the defender
of the group. Here are a few lines that sum up his position and
suggest its tone at the time of *Critique et vérité:*

> Certain books of criticism have, then, come into existence,
> offering themselves to be read in the same ways as works
> that are literary, properly speaking, although the authors of
> these books are, as to official status, only critics and not
> writers. If the new criticism has some reality, it is there: not
> in the unity of its methods, even less in the snobbism,
> which—it is convenient to say—sustains it, but in the
> solitude of the critical act, affirmed henceforth, far from the
> alibis of science or of institutions, as a deliberate act of *writ-
> ing* in the full sense of that word (*un acte de pleine
> écriture*). Formerly separated by the worn-out myth of the
> "proud creator and the humble servant, both necessary, with
> each in his place, etc.," the writer and the critic now meet
> in the same difficult situation, facing the same object: lan-
> guage. (p. 46)

In 1967, one year after *Critique et vérité*, Barthes published
a substantial volume called *Système de la mode*. A work of applied semiology, it is a study of fashion clothing, more specifically, of language used in certain fashion magazines (*Elle, Jar-
din des modes, Echo de la mode*, and *Vogue*). Barthes had
already noted, in his *Eléments de sémiologie* of 1964, the possi-

bility of using the Saussurian distinction of *langue-parole*, language-speech, in matters of clothing, food, automobiles, and furniture. Though not exactly light reading, *Système de la mode* has agreeable ironic and even sarcastic overtones as it applies to the clichés of fashion-writing terms like "denotation," "connotation," "syntagma," "metalanguage," "matrix," "transformation," and "simultaneous systems." In and through the technicalities of his analysis one can see distinct movement toward the method he applies in *S/Z* (1970), his most significant single work of criticism.

In an interview with Raymond Bellour (*Les Lettres françaises*, May 20, 1970), Barthes was asked: "In your view, what is represented by the experience of *S/Z*, the title of which, like a witticism, symbolizes the work of reading that you carried out on a not very well-known story by Balzac: *Sarrasine?*" Barthes replied:

> I must say, in the first place, that in the year when I began to write the *Sarrasine* episode—the seminar that I gave at the Ecole pratique des hautes études, then the book that followed it—was perhaps the densest and happiest of my working life. I had the exalting impression that I was attacking something really new, in the strict sense of the term, that is, which had never been done. For a long time, in order to advance the structural analysis of narrative I had wanted to devote myself to a micro-analysis, an analysis that would be patient and progressive, but not exhaustive, because there can be no question of exhausting all [possible] senses: a perpetual analysis, as one might speak of a perpetual calendar. . . . The experience of *S/Z* represents for me,

above everything else, a pleasure, a delight (*jouissance*) in work and writing.

He has said more specifically elsewhere that what he has attempted in *S/Z* is to "write a reading" (*écrire une lecture*) (*Figaro littéraire*, March 9–15, 1970). "Has it never happened to you," he asks, "to stop constantly while reading, not for lack of interest, but, on the contrary because of a flood of ideas, of stimulations, of associations? . . . It is that kind of reading, disrespectful because it cuts up the text, and fascinated, loving (*éprise*) because it returns to it and feeds on it, that I have tried to write."

Sarrasine, a sculptor with a name that sounds feminine in French, falls in love with a beautiful singer, a *castrato*, whom he believes to be a woman. When he finds out the truth, he feels degraded, tries to kill the man and to break up the statue he has made of him. Then, a *castrato* himself in a symbolic sense, Sarrasine dies by the hand of an assassin. One would expect the name Sarrasine to be spelled with a Z, a letter whose very shape, according to Barthes, connotes a "stinging, castrating whip"; the Z has disappeared from his name, censored, like his own desire for castration, but it reappears in the name of the singer, Zambinella. The bar that separates the S of Sarrasine and the Z of Zambinella signifies the unbridgeable gap between them and also, of course, the work of the psychic censor.

As one might expect, the outer shape of this written-reading is unusual. The Balzac story has been cut into 561 numbered fragments (with Arabic numerals), varying in length from one word to five or six lines. After each fragment come a few lines of commentary, printed in small type; and then, interpolated in this sequence running from 1 through 561, are 103 numbered digressions (with Roman numerals), printed in large type, and amounting in each case to a page or two of text. In an appendix the story is reprinted without interruption. In another appendix the digressions are integrated by number into an outline, a *Table raisonnée*, so that the reader can see at a glance, although it depends somewhat on how good he is at glances, how the topics of the digressions fit into a logical scheme.

Among the principles in the back of Barthes's mind as he starts to work on *Sarrasine* are three that seem to me fundamental. (1) The first concerns the plural aspect of literary texts. The aim in interpretation is not to arrive at a single, exclusive sense (that much we know from *Critique et vérité*), but to grasp and appreciate the plural (*le pluriel*) of which the text is composed. Here Barthes's thinking appears to have evolved considerably. He posits, as a limiting case, an ideal text that is *infinitely* plural and contrasts with it the classical text (*le texte classique*), which is characterized by a limited or, as he says, *parsimonious* plurality of sense. There is a long sentence describing the ideal text that I shall quote, translating as best I can Barthes's abundant, at times baroque, style:

> Let us pose first of all the image of a triumphant plural which is not impoverished by any constraint of representation (of imitation). In this ideal text, the networks are multiple with an interplay among them, such that no network dominates the others; this text is a galaxy of signifiers, not a

structure of signifieds; it has no beginning; it is reversible;
one has access to it by several entries, none of which can be
declared with certainty to be the principal one; the codes
that it mobilizes extend their profiles as far as one can see
—they are undecidable (the sense is never submitted to a
decisive principle, unless it be by a throw of dice): systems
of sense may take hold of this absolutely plural text, but the
number of these systems is never closed, having as their measure the infinite of language. (pp. 11–12)

This ideal text has no exterior to be outlined; it has no totality: insofar as we can speak of narrative structure or of narrative grammar and logic apropos of a text, we are concerned
with incomplete or parsimonious plurality. It is important to
note that this is, as mentioned above, an ideal, but also that it is
part of a historical trend. As Barthes looks back over the history of French literature, he sees *textes classiques*—of limited
plurality—from the seventeenth century through Romanti-
cism, until in fact about 1850, when the modern text (*le texte
moderne*), attracted by the infinite play of sense and senses,
began to appear. And of course, *Sarrasine*, the Balzac story
under consideration, belongs to the former category of classical texts.

(2) The second principle follows from the fact that the
objective of the reader/interpreter is the plural aspect of his
text. What can he use as his prospecting instrument, his divin-
ing rod? The answer is: *connotation*. A full account of what
Barthes means by that term would make a story too long to be
told here. He defines it in a number of ways (the following adverbs are literal translations): "definitionally," "topically," "an-

alytically," "topologically," "semiologically," "dynamically," "functionally," "structurally," and "ideologically." Some idea of what he means can be gathered from these lines where he writes "definitionally":

> [A connotation] is a determination, a relation, an anaphora, a trait having the power to refer to earlier, later, or exterior items that have been mentioned, to other places in the text, or to some other text; we must not restrict in any way this relation, except by not confusing connotation with the association of ideas: the latter sends us back to the system of a subject; the former is a correlation immanent in the text or texts; or again, if you will, it is an association made by the text as subject within its own system. (pp. 14–15)

(3) In the third place, as he prepares for the step-by-step analysis of *Sarrasine*, Barthes has in mind a special notion of the status that any particular text has. It is not to be thought of as embodying some ideal structure; it does not give access by induction to a model which then explains the example. Rather, *it is one entry into the network that is all of literature.* "La littérature elle-même n'est jamais qu'un seul texte" (p. 19), he says, and in the context he means that all of literature, past, present, and future, is no more (nor less!) than a single, unbounded text. Therefore to work on *a* text is to enter *the* text; to analyze *Sarrasine* is to enter a vast perspective whose vanishing point is not and can never be fixed.

What do these principles lead to in practice? As I have pointed out, Barthes cuts the text—the line formed by the text, so to speak—into 561 segments or *lexies*. An absolutely essential notion appears after Barthes has commented on details in the first three fragments: that of *code*. Since he is observing and pondering the behavior of signs, of meanings, of connotations in his text, he needs some means of drawing them together: a code is, precisely, that which groups the separate items into sequences and configurations. Moreover, in the first three *lexies*, consisting of the title and first sentence of the story, *five* codes are visible, and since this list appears to be exhaustive, the implication is that every item to be commented on will fall under one of these headings, take its place in one of these systems of meaning. There one has, I think, the main point of the rich and ingenious analyses, always interesting, sometimes irritating, contained in *S/Z:* it is a study of the emergence and interweaving of codes, seen in and through the text.

There is a hermeneutic code, for references to the unraveling of the plot, in this case, the identity of Zambinella; a semantic code, for traits attached to persons mainly, but sometimes to places or things; a proaïretic code (Barthes is fond of neologisms based on Greek roots), for choices and sequences of actions; a cultural code, for citations of received wisdom; a symbolic code or field, the place par excellence of multivalence and reversibility, marked in this story by the breakdown of distinctions and antitheses, by disorder in meanings, sexes, and fortunes.

These codes form a kind of network through which the text passes, or out of which it comes; without them there could be no text. Barthes deliberately does very little to systematize the codes internally or to order them with reference to each other. In fact, his purpose is much less to show a structure or struc-

tures than to begin five inventories of elements and to point to
a process of structuration. The result is not an "interpretation"
of *Sarrasine* (except in some very loose meaning of the word);
it is not at all like Barthes's interpretation of the tragedies of
Racine, which was a discursive account, an essay on Racinian
anthropology, as he called it, standing in sharp opposition to
other accounts or interpretations. Without mentioning his earlier work and the controversy it aroused, Barthes nonetheless
seems quite clear about the difference between *an* interpretation and his present work, which offers a way of thinking
about interpretation and furnishes an elaborate prelude to interpretations, in the plural. As he says:

> We shall not expound the criticism of a text or a criticism of
> this text; we shall propose the semantic material (divided up
> but not distributed) of several criticisms (psychological, psy-
> choanalytic, thematic, historical, structural); it is up to each
> critic then (if he so desires) to play, to make his voice heard,
> which is [i.e., means] listening to one of the voices of the
> text. What we are trying to do is to sketch the stereographic
> space of a writing (*une écriture*). (p. 21)

That passage suggests that we ought to pay some attention
to the imagery that sustains Barthes's reflection. Each of the
codes is a voice; the crossing and blending of voices is the very
activity of writing; and the product of that activity is the text.
From the image of voice or voices to that of music and polyph-
ony is only a short step, and Barthes takes it. His divisions
of the text, his *lexies*, correspond to measures; and using musi-
cal notation, he even makes up something like a score for the

first thirteen measures or fragments, with lines for the codes and passing allusions to brasses, percussion, woodwinds, and strings. However, his most insistent image is that of plaiting and weaving, the production of tresses, lace, fabrics. After comparing at length the working of the hermeneutic code to the activity of the lacemaker, Barthes generalizes:

> This process holds for the entire text. The codes taken together (*l'ensemble des codes*), as soon as they are drawn into the work, into the movement of reading, constitute a tress (text, tissue, and tress are all the same thing); every thread, every code is a voice; these voices, tressed or tressing, form the writing (*écriture*); alone the voice does no work, it transforms nothing: it *expresses*, but as soon as the hand intervenes to assemble and mingle the inert threads, there is working, there is transformation. (p. 166)

The concept of code and the imagery surrounding it throw a great deal of light on what seem to be some of Barthes's central intuitions. One persistent idea in his work has been the turning of culture into nature. I mean that he has seen and sought to question decisively the general human tendency to think that what is before us, what is about us, what we do and say as a matter of course—to think that all that is innocent, natural. We carelessly turn *what is by culture* into *what must be by nature*. Hence the necessity to get beneath the surface of behavior and language, in order to see how that transformation occurs. The notion of sign, which allies itself easily with a distrust of surfaces and of face-values, provides him with the key. Everywhere Barthes looks he sees men making signs, attaching meanings to signifiers; the science of signs, semiology, can presumably reduce this process to rule and order, and at the same time, show the true relation between nature and culture. Moreover, there is an intellectual method that corresponds perfectly to that complex of intuitions: logistic, analysis and recombination, discovery of primitive elements and of the ways by which they enter into structures and sequences that become ever larger and longer.

In literature, to be specific, he looks below the smooth surface—apparently innocent, natural, final—and discovers signs, that is, discontinuous and primitive elements. These signifiers and signifieds call to each other and even have systematic relations to each other, and so they cluster into codes or systems like the five that underlie the voices he hears in the story by Balzac; these codes or systems, these threadlike or chainlike elements, may in turn be tressed into a text; and every text takes its place, with every other text, in the total fabric that is literature.

That sounds and is, I think, quite mechanistic, but Barthes has found a way to animate the machine. His main concern has shifted from structure to structuration, seen as an autonomous activity with a life of its own, almost independent of men, for, as he has said, man is no longer the center of structures. This shift he connects to a change in emphasis in linguistics from problems of taxonomy to problems of generation and transformation.

Again, as a means of counteracting simplistic formulas that might emerge in a theory that seems to begin and end with elements and syntax, Barthes plays still another trump card, the notion of the infinite, of the *infini du langage*. I think it is the presence of this term in his argument that accounts for the slight feeling of dizziness induced occasionally by *S/Z*. In his famous fragment on the disproportion of man and nature, Pascal produces a similar sensation with two infinites—the infinitely large and the infinitely small, with uneasy man somewhere in between. Unless I am mistaken, Barthes confronts us with *three* infinites: one's native language, the linguistic ocean from which the signs of literature are drawn; the codes, which have no distinct boundaries or limits; and literature itself, the text with a capital *T*, which stretches without end behind and before us as an orderly process, an interlace of signs.

One way of saying to ourselves what, in general, Barthes is doing in *Critique et vérité* and *S/Z* is to trace out what happens to some critical reflexes—our own, perhaps—when they encounter this radical decision to discuss literature in the context of sign-theory. (1) If it is our bent to imagine the *author* as a unique person, full of experience and fortified by an art of expression, who freely brings into being objects that otherwise would never have existed, we must be prepared for a challenge: Barthes rejects the idea of a psychological and moral subject with something to say; for him the author is empty, a paper being, inscribed in the work but not determining it, and not having over it any right of property. (2) If we incline to the view of the literary *work* as made up in some way, simple or subtle, of two elements or levels, content and form, or if, in place of that, we opt for the work as a whole consisting of organically related parts, we are in for another shock: Barthes proposes to us not works but texts, that is, tissues of signs derived from codes, chains of signifiers and signifieds having no limits or centers that merge, in fact, into a single Text held together (at least in its essential tendency) by a dreamlike logic of the intemporal, the reversible, the interchangeable. (3) If, again, we find ourselves conceiving of the *reader-critic* as a kind of consumer of literature, first passive and then reactive, either moving toward a judgment of what the author has offered or joining him in his way of seeing himself and the world, we are brought up short by Barthes's assertions: for him the reader has an extraordinarily active role to play; he is a producer, not a consumer, of meanings; he is, himself, a system of meanings and codes; by microanalysis he discovers structures and watches them move into and out of his field of view; and most important of all, he writes as well as reads, trying always to tie his mode of discourse into the circuits resonating in the original text. (4) If, finally, we adopt—on the example of some ancient and neo-classical critics—the thesis that literary works have as their *aim* or *effect* some kind of instructing, moving, and pleasing (taken together or in some combination and preferably redefined so as to save our vocabulary from too-close association with that of oratory), we collide once again with the position of Barthes: having pulverized the work *as such*, he makes of it the means whereby we may enter a process of using and transforming signs; we shall no doubt be instructed, moved, and pleased in the peculiar way that semiology makes possible; but we must realize, by a Copernican leap, that we are not the center of this activity; we do not constitute it—we are born into it; we do not

select it—it selects us; and so the effect of the text is finally
to draw us into the infinitely permutative play of subjectless
language.

Another and less paradoxical way of saying what Roland
Barthes does is to speak of disciplines rather than of topics.
Here we find that we cannot answer the question without defining the relationship of his enterprise to *science*. He has for a
long time and in various degrees thought of himself as a
sémiologue, a semiologist; and he has often affirmed the value
of Freudian psychology (especially as continued by Jacques
Lacan). But he insists on maintaining a certain distance between himself and science, while at the same time making free
and inventive use of its concepts and techniques. In an interview in *Les Lettres Françaises* (March 2, 1967) published when
the *Système de la mode* appeared, he made the point very
clearly:

> The status of science constitutes a problem for me, and I am
> far from having on this point the same position as the other
> structuralists. That no doubt arises from the fact that my
> object of study is literature. . . . I am trying to specify
> (*préciser*) scientific procedures, to test them more or less, but
> never to end them with a conclusion (*clausule*) that is typi-
> cally scientific, because literary science cannot in any case
> or in any fashion have the last word about literature.

Later in the same interview, after saying that he now speaks
less of science and its metalanguages than he used to, he adds:

> When I write, it seems to me that I seek to establish a cer-
> tain play (*jeu*) with science, an activity of disguised parody.

> I believe more and more that the profound movement of the
> critic is [toward] the destruction of metalanguage . . .
> [scientific] objectivity is merely one field of images among
> others. . . . As far as *critical* metalanguage is concerned, one
> can only get around it by instituting a sort of isomorphism
> between the language of literature and discourse about liter-
> ature. The science of literature is literature.

The simultaneous affirmation and denial of science and the
effort to overcome the separation of literature and criticism
give us two important clues. *Science* does not preside over his
work; at crucial moments it gives way to *dialectic*. But the dialectic of Barthes is not metaphysical in scope; it always
emerges against a background of *history*—Marxist history,
freely interpreted—which fixes the terms in which contradictions are stated and sometimes resolved. Finally, science, dialectic, and history (which I do not intend to place here in a
strict order of precedence: one of the difficulties in achieving a
satisfactory approximation to Barthes's views comes from the
ease with which he travels back and forth among disciplines)
—these perspectives are subordinated to what he likes to call
écriture, writing, or as I think we may call it without injustice,
rhetoric. Not rhetoric in some reduction to combative or flow-
ery speech, of course; I mean rhetoric as eclectic culture, commitment to language, operational attitude, effective force. Although his work is focused mainly on the interpretation of
literature, he offers it in all its phases and moments as a contribution to bringing in a freer way of thinking and feeling than
we now know. But we must not oversimplify. "I should like to
be a writer," he said in 1970, and as the context shows, he

meant by that not someone for whom language is only an instrument, but someone who accepts language as a fateful milieu in which one lives and moves; in this approach to sign and sense, insofar as a writer is a force and, indeed, is at all, *he is his language*.

FRANK KERMODE
The Use of the Codes

> . . . the great problem is to outplay the
> *signifié*, to outplay law, to outplay the
> father, to outplay the repressed.
> —Roland Barthes [1]

𝓜 Y TITLE IS CAPABLE of two interpretations, so I
had better explain what I mean to write about. The
codes are those of Roland Barthes's *S/Z*, but I do not intend
to offer detailed discussion of what he calls his "stereographic"
method of textual analysis. My concern is less with the how
than with the why. The codes may come to be recognized as
an interesting advance on the Neo-formalist descriptive techniques which preceded their invention, though that they will
hardly do so without considerable modification is my belief,
but not my present theme. I am interested in the normative aspect. Barthes, let us remind ourselves, is dealing with the kind
of text he calls *lisible*, distinguished from the authentically
modern *scriptible* text by the fact that it is not indefinitely
open to "production" by the reader. *Lisible* texts are said to

[1] From an interview with Stephen Heath in *Signs of the Times*,
ed. S. Heath, C. McCabe, and C. Prendergast (Cambridge, n.d.
[1971]), p. 49.

have a limited degree of plurality and are subject to various kinds of closure. Barthes investigates the way we read such texts, and in so doing indicates their limitations—as to restricted plurality and closure—by comparison with ideal modern texts which have neither.

St. Augustine explained, in his book *The City of God*, that "those things which have no significance of their own are interwoven for the sake of things which are significant," and Barthes is making a not wholly dissimilar point when he observes that "there is text everywhere . . . but not everything is text." [2] St. Augustine's expression retains some relevance to the way novels are written and read, with this important qualification: unlike us he was quite certain about which things were significant and which not. Lacking that assurance, we have to assume that narratives capable of interesting competent readers are likely to be in some ways inexplicit and indeterminable to the extent that there is no universal agreement as to what kinds of significance, if any, are to be attributed to any particular moment of a text; so there is in effect, in all such cases, an indefinite measure of plurality. If it were not so teachers of literature would soon work themselves out of jobs. Whatever Professor Raymond Picard may think, most of them have long assumed the plurality of the texts they choose to study.

There can obviously be new ways of talking about this interesting situation, but they can hardly succeed if they also pretend to have invented it. That the reading of a novel is a highly individualized performance by the reader, its virtue de-

[2] *Signs of the Times*, p. 51.

pending upon his competence, is surely common knowledge, and I doubt if Stendhal thought he was proclaiming a new truth when he compared the novel to the bow and the reader to the violin.[3] This analogy falters, of course, since novels, unlike fiddles, can nudge and prompt. It is also true that readers of restricted competence can allow themselves, as it were, to be played by the novel. The mere existence of a story-line, and the more or less traditional devices by which a text can pretend to establish the authenticity of its account of the world, can ensure the abandonment of strenuous analytic activity. There are banal performances and there are also banal novels; but literary critics (competent readers, we hope) like the works they like precisely because performances are possible which are not banal, and which, moreover, may be indefinitely various, not only as between readers but also as between readings.

It will be observed that I have already begun to "recuperate" the Barthian codes. Of the five, two are what he calls "irreversible": the hermeneutic and the proaïretic, the voice of truth and the voice of the empirical. It is true that people really do like to see how it all comes out, and like to think it's real. Insofar as this is the case, the linear codes do account for a restriction on plurality,[4] an appeal to passive consumption.

[3] "Un roman est comme un archet; la caisse du violon qui rend les sons, c'est l'âme du lecteur." (*Henri Brûlard*, quoted by Stephen Gilman, "Meditations on a Stendhalian Metaphor," in *Interpretation: Theory and Practice*, ed. Charles S. Singleton (Baltimore, 1969), p. 155.

[4] "Ce qui bloque la reversibilité violà ce qui limite le pluriel du texte classique. Ces blocages ont des noms: c'est d'une part la

There is, however, a possibility of a problematical use of these codes. This is a possibility Barthes is unwilling to consider, except as deviation from the norm of the *lisible;* instead he invents his antithetical (but empty) category, the *scriptible* text, which would be a galaxy of signifiers with no signifieds. Such a text, he says, would be rather like an onion, whereas the texts of the *lisible,* which always *close* on something, offer at best an apricot. There is a stone or pit of content.[5]

How does the *lisible* come by the limited measure of plurality it has? Barthes does not allow that there is any hierarchy in the codes, but it is clear from his demonstration of the method that the symbolic code is much the most important, for, aside from the linear codes, the cultural code is what he calls *endoxal* (referring to vulgar knowledge, opinion, ideology) and the semic is concerned with the obsolete notions of character and theme. Whatever it is that may redeem the classic—make it somehow anticipate the modern—seems to arise in the symbolic code. In the Balzac story he analyzes (*Sarrasine*),

---

vérité et d'autre part l'empirie: ce précisément contre quoi—ou entre quoi—s'établit le texte moderne." Roland Barthes, *S/Z* (Paris, 1970), p. 37.

   [5] ". . . if up until now we have looked at the text as a species of fruit with a kernel (an apricot, for example), the flesh being the form and the pit the content, it would be better to see it as an onion, a construction of layers (or levels, or systems) whose body contains, finally, no heart, no kernel, no secret, no irreducible principle, nothing except the infinity of its own envelopes—which envelopes nothing other than the unity of its own surfaces." Roland Barthes, "Style and Its Image," in *Literary Style: A Symposium,* ed. Seymour Chatman (New York, 1971), p. 10.

it is the means by which a classic narrative may say more than it knows, for instance by elaborating symbolic themes related to castration and money. And only when it both says more than it knows and contrives to bring into question the validity of the assumptions on which it was written can the classic text find its only value: as a prophecy of the modern. As Philippe Sollers remarks, the classic text is "an economized plural. . . . It does not have to take account of the fact that it is written. . . . The classic text . . . is a fetish, a chimera that half-speaks. It spirals round a barred empty subject." It is this emptiness, which the classics, except in their moments of prophetic unease, suppose to be plenitude, that the modern would acknowledge and exhibit. The best the *lisible* can do is, more or less by accident, to offer us the chance to let it escape from its habitual representation of "life" as "a nauseous compound of general opinions" [6] and provide the reader with something he can, as Barthes says, *write*, that is to say, read creatively, "produce."

We must consider what is implied by this doctrine of the ambiguous innocence of the classical text. The *lisible*, it appears, assumes that its relation to the world is one of specularity, or of transparence; the text pretends to be absent—as if, to recall Coleridge's invaluable expression, it had been defecated to a pure transparency. This is the basis of Barthes's distinction between *écrivance* (classic, transparent) and *écriture* (modern, announcing its difference, a text among texts). People who believe in the simple specularity and transparency of nov-

[6] Philippe Sollers, "Reading *S/Z*," in *Signs of the Times*, p. 40.

els are indeed very naïve, and they are certainly prevented by
their simplicity from reading texts in their textuality, narratives
in their narrativity, and so on. (Any acceptable notion of competence would presumably exclude them.) And inasmuch as
lisible texts pretend to accept these myths, they have to be
subjected to a process of deconstruction before their authentic
though limited pluralities become available to the modern
reader or producer; what is more, they must offer, in spite of
themselves, opportunities for the application of these procedures.

We can now approach the central issues. For Barthes, the
only hope for *lisible* texts is that they allow themselves, in limited ways, to be treated as modern. He is always quite explicit
about his modernism, longing for mutatory texts to make us
even more modern than we already are, to take us beyond the
point of the last great mutation, associated with Mallarmé. The
notion of the great historical mutation, which has dominated
so much of Anglo-Saxon criticism in this century, happens in
France to take this form: the crucial date is often given as
1870, give or take a year or two; and after that time no text
ought to be naïvely unaware of its own existence as something
written. Nor should it, considered as a fruit, possess a stone.
All closure is in bad faith. The modern "galaxy of signifiers"
would have nothing to signify, or rather it would be in constant circulation and signifying ceaselessly, "mais sans
délégation à un grand ensemble final, à une structure
dernière." [7] To put it crudely, the *lisible* is *about* something, it
refers to some validating plot within it. One reason why

[7] *S/Z*, p. 18.

Barthes gave up the Formalist attempt to establish a narrative *langue* of which every *récit* is a *parole* is precisely his fear that success in that operation would revive the old organicist myth of a structure peculiar to a particular work. Thus the work we wanted to open up would close again, again possess a signified secret. Such closure he would condemn as ideological, the consequence of false assumptions, occidental and endoxal, about the nature of signs. Our business as moderns is to read in order to maximize plurality, not in order to understand secrets. The apricot stone must go. We must not seek to discover structures but to produce structurations. Neither the Formalist nor the organicist model will serve: "il faut à la fois dégager le texte de son extérieure et de sa totalité." [8] Japanese *vides*, not European *pleins*—oriental onions, not occidental apricots —are what we require. And we can protect ourselves against story (which dishonestly claims to reveal truth) and against specularity which is naïve and dishonest, and against all the other threats. We have semiological defenses; we know that our bourgeois culture habitually transforms history into nature by imposing on us myths of various kinds; [9] and so we should not be so simple as to believe in narrative structures, even when texts pretend to have them, or in bogus closures. Our motto: "Point de dieu, de verité, de morale *au fond* de ces signifiants." [10]

[8] *Ibid.*, p. 12.

[9] The theme of Barthes's essay "Le mythe, aujourd'hui," *Mythologies* (Paris, 1957).

[10] Roland Barthes, *L'Empire des Signes* (Geneva, 1970), Barthes's jacket note.

We might once more ask whether Barthes, with rather extravagant (and for that matter, ideological) additions, is not saying something that in a way we know already. But a more urgent question is, what do novels themselves know about all this? Can it be said that the *lisible* novel solemnly refuses (save when its composure is betrayed by some accident in the symbolic code) to consider skeptical enquiries as to whether it has a stone or not?

Let us look at a novel which may help us to answer this question. It may be objected that a better example would be a much older novel than Anthony Burgess's *MF*, and that I am cheating by choosing a book which is modern, and problematical in ways that suit my purpose. It would be quite easy to meet this objection by speaking instead of *The Scarlet Letter*, for example, a work which would give Barthes a lot of trouble. But Burgess's novel happens to raise the whole issue in a simpler way, and it is undoubtedly what Barthes would call *lisible*; it is not even a *nouveau roman*; it has linear codings and closure. And I think it neatly illustrates the point that non-*scriptible* texts are perfectly capable of being the sort of fruit that can ask whether it contains a stone or not.

Miles Faber, a clever lad, quick with polyglot puns, addicted to word-games of all kinds and especially riddles, has a rage for disorder. As a protest against order, the past, the dividedness of the world, and so forth, he copulates, on the steps of his college library, with a girl called Miss Tukang. We meet him in New York, discussing this event with his father's lawyer, a Mr. Loewe, the first of a polyglot pride of lions in the book. Mr. Loewe is charged by Miles's father to prevent him from visiting the Caribbean island of Castita, where he wishes to study the works of a neglected but great anti-artist called Sib Legeru. His father's secret motive is a horror of incest. He has arranged for his son to marry a Chinese girl, seeing in miscegenation the greatest obtainable measure of exogamy. And since Miles's sister is in Castita, he must be kept away from there.

Miles is staying at the Algonquin. He enjoys a new soft drink, sold in owl-shaped bottles and called Coca-Coho. He dreams of owls. After many adventures, he evades Loewe and flies to Miami. There another leonine representative of his father (Pardeleos) asks his views on incest. Freedom-loving, rational Miles says he thinks it permissible in principle; but in the absence of absolutely dependable contraceptives he would not, for medical reasons, practice it. When Pardeleos informs him that he, Miles, is the product of an incestuous union, he understands why he suffers from certain minor ailments.

After sailing through a storm which casts some doubt on the proposition that all disorder is good, he reaches Castita, only to find himself in a situation of apparently irrational complexity. There is a circus, Fonanta's circus, with a female Welsh bird-trainer, who seems to recognize Miles. A lionlike cripple, a sphinx, having moralized on man as "the great unifier of disparates," asks him a riddle, to be answered on pain of death. He refuses to answer, and saves himself by blowing a football referee's whistle, which he has found, together with the rulebook of soccer, in his hotel (a notion picked up, I daresay, from *Heart of Darkness*). He discovers that he has a foulmouthed obscene double, an unknown twin son of the birdwoman Av-

eryn (Welsh for "birds"); and when, in searching for the
works of Sib Legeru, he runs into his sister, he finds himself
under the necessity of saving her from rape by this double, at
whose death he then presides. To save himself from her ven-
geance he must now convince the birdwoman that he is her missing son, and the only way he can do this is by undertaking to
marry his sister.

The circus, as it happens, has a riddling priest among its
clowns, and he marries the siblings, amidst the din of circus
bands and animals and the insults of the performers, who hate
the young man they take Miles to be. Dr. Fonanta, owner of
the circus, arrives to bestow his blessing, regretting only that
there is no eclipse that night. Taking his bride to bed under
surveillance, Miles just manages not to consummate his union;
but there is another trial in store. The birdwoman has talking
birds who ask riddles, and hunting birds (all named after living
English novelists) who hunt. She puts Miles's identity to a final
test by requiring him to answer a riddle set by a talking bird
on pain of having his eyes pecked out by the hawks. He survives, by using his whistle, escapes, and marries the Chinese
girl. He finally turns out to be a black man, from Cardiff,
Wales.

This is a simplified account of a much more agitated jostle of
events, puzzles, riddles, jokes, connections, and disconnections.
MF looks like a difficult book to systematize. Lest we should
think it a merely random medley of picaresque detail, it offers
a few hints about its structure, many of them vouchsafed by
Dr. Fonanta himself. Some riddles, it appears, should remain
unanswered, however simple; especially if asked by sphinxes,
themselves riddles. "The riddler has to be itself a riddle. But

no, the ultimate organic creation's emissary rather, granted a voice. With this voice it says: *Dare to disturb the mystery of the universe.* For order has both to be challenged and not to be challenged, this being the anomalous condition of the sustention of the cosmos. Exogamy means disruption and also stability; incest means stability and also disruption." The harder you try to avoid incest, by randomness, the more you are likely to commit it. For example, Tukang is Malayan for "skilled workman" (*faber*). Z. Fonanta—*zoon phonanta*, the speaking animal—is man, product of incest, inventor of the archetypal sign-system, language. Siblegeru, pseudonym of Fonanta, is Old English for incest; and there is, even in his works, a banal order, for the speaking animal cannot avoid it. Fonanta also explains that not all of Miles's explanations, systematizations, were correct; some were insignificant, some were unsystematic, coincidences; not all were texts.

Miles finally exhorts us not to answer the riddle of the book. Abandon this impassioned decoding, he says, cease to limit pluralities. And apart from the explanations the book itself offers, and which I've sketched in, it seems to be mostly random inventions and riddling fantasies. It makes ambiguous claims for order without apparently having much of it—it has a touch of Siblegeru.

Yet the book is much more closed than appears on the surface. The secret is that one needs to distinguish "that which belongs to the order of structure and that which belongs to the order of event"; [11] and the author of that formula, Claude Lévi-Strauss, provides more specific aids. He believes that the

[11] Claude Lévi-Strauss, *The Scope of Anthropology* (London, 1967), p. 30.

incest prohibition is universal, and the *sine qua non* of social organization. Its universality entails, given the model he employs, the existence of identifiable transformations of the Oedipus myth. One such is the Algonquin myth of a girl who suffered attempted rape by the double of her brother, who kills the attacker, and is then required to establish to the mother of the victim that he is her son. She happens to be a mistress of owls (called "Coco-cohu" in Algonquin). The young man tries to mislead her by marrying his sister, but there is another test, as a consequence of which the woman is fooled; the birds aren't, but he escapes. "The very precautions taken to avoid incest make it unavoidable." [12]

Oedipus is himself a double (supposed dead but living), and thus far there is correlation between the two myths. But what about the Sphinx's riddle? Riddles are extremely rare in Amerindian cultures. However, it happens that in Algonquin myth owls ask riddles that must be answered under pain of death. Further, the Pueblo Indians have ceremonial clowns, themselves thought to be the products of incestuous unions. The correlation is complete. Puzzles and riddles, like incest, bring together elements that ought to be kept apart. There are many more transformations; for instance, these myths are transformations of the Parsifal myth. When the Indian hero gives the right answer the eternal winter ends; when Parsifal asks the right question the land is renewed. Chastity is related to the answer that lacks a question, incest is related to the question that lacks an answer (and however simple, better unanswered). The Algonquin-Oedipus myths invert Parsifal;

[12] *Ibid.*

incestuous unions engender not spring but storms and fermentation and decay (as in the noisome works of Sib Legeru and in the joint of beef Miles cooks for his fat sugar-loving sister).

Certainly this seems to weld contradictions, reduces dispersity. And it's only a beginning. There is more—enough to create, though perhaps only in the naïve or incompetent, the notion that the book is laying down the law about the world. Zoon Fonanta is incestuous because any myth of human origin must be either that, or demonic; but his descendants, the Fabers, are programmed for system-making, and should therefore avoid incest. Their business is with the perception or invention of systematic relations homologous with language—which is to say: their business is to be human. The Jakobsonian triangles which chart our learning to speak also chart our cooking. Culturally, cooking is the avoidance of incest between organic matter and the sun, and the avoidance of a rottenness that would destroy the world. The random is systematized by the mere presence of Miles, as when he throws away the rotten meat; or when honey and tobacco are reconciled in Miss Emmett's brand of cigarettes, Honeydew; or when Miss Emmett attacks the double's genitals with scissors and there is, Miles notes, a rare collocation of three dual forms, scissors, trousers, ballocks. The wedding of Miles and his sister is accompanied by a charivari—an ancient European way of making an offensive demonstration against a marriage considered for some reason—disparity of age, or undue consanguinity—reprehensible. The same noises that signal a charivari are made at eclipses. Eclipses also signify a disruption, cosmological but analogous to the social; the unsuitable marriage and the

eclipse alike interfere with the ordinary rhythmical processes
of human life—with that cycle of season, love, friendship,
and so on, which Fonanta squarely commends to the disgusted
Miles, as preferable to the stinking chaos of Sib. Lévi-Strauss
cites a myth, found, he says, all over America, that links
eclipses, rotting meat, disease, and incest.[13] Without the tabu
on incest (of which Miles's genetic arguments are merely a
minor reinforcement) there could be no order, no human
system-making.

I do not think we can dismiss this text as a mere fantasy on
themes of Lévi-Strauss. Of course it is partly a matter of jokes
—the naming of the hawks for English novelists is not only a
private joke (who is Anthony?) but a comment on a passage in
Edmund Leach's book which attacks the French anthropolo-
gist for being very un-English about the naming of animals.[14]
But more serious questions arise. That the *structure* of the
book makes sense only in terms of Lévi-Strauss's work must
seem important. Lévi-Strauss thinks the transformations he describes are close to the essence of humanity: "There is a simultaneous production of the myths themselves, by the mind
which generates them; and by the myths, of an image of the
world which is already inherent in the structure of the mind.
By taking its raw material from nature, mythic thought pro-

[13] Claude Lévi-Strauss, *The Raw and the Cooked* (London,
1970), p. 296, trans. J. and D. Weightman from *Le Cru et le Cuit*
(Paris, 1964).
[14] Edmund Leach, *Lévi-Strauss* (London, 1970), pp. 88 ff. The
reference is to a passage in Lévi-Strauss's *La Pensée Sauvage*
(Paris, 1962).

ceeds in the same way as language, which chooses phonemes from among the natural sounds of which a practically unlimited range is to be found in childish babbling." [15] We live in the world by making such systems of meaning; this involves things which have and things which have not significance, though in translating nature into culture man acts in such a way that the discrete and paradigmatic do not abolish the continuous. Does *MF*, by encoding material Lévi-Strauss decoded, naïvely endorse all that he says? Certainly its mythic universe sets us another problem: what to do with the material, sometimes deliberately planted, which we cannot on these terms encode (like the revelation that Miles is a black man, or that his solution of the first riddle was wrong)?

And this may only be part of a larger problem: what happens to this novel if we accept the quite common opinion that Lévi-Strauss is all wrong? Burgess seems to think of man as a being who "hammers away at structures"—certainly *he* does, and so do other writers. His structures include much that deceives us in our attempts to read paradigmatically—some things which we may miss, others which he might have missed (since it is true that the reader speaks in the text, though perhaps not, as Barthes claims, the reader alone).[16] In this writer's text we may, if we choose, read a message. The speaking animal, condemned to the avoidance of incest, is constitutionally a system-maker. Zoon Fonanta invents language, Miles Faber invents homologous meaning-systems. The book in which they appear denies that it is a mere agglutination of random ele-

[15] *The Raw and the Cooked*, p. 341.
[16] "Dans le texte, seul parle le lecteur." *S/Z*, p. 157.

ments; it speaks of order and the threat to it of anticultural disorder. It could be called culturally conservative. It speaks of how structures arise; and it suggests a deeper center from which they arise. The detail of the book is generated from this structure; to put this another way, there is a model exterior to the text which must be known if the book is to be explained or closed.

However, the rightness or wrongness of that model is not the point. The book is an example of ways of meaning-making, and yet strongly criticizes them; thus its structure is self-questioning. It is strongly implied that reading a novel is a process quite like, and sharing the dangers of, solving riddles: one finds the codes, distinguishes information from noise, plays the indeterminable game of syntagm and paradigm which is the origin of all plural readings. Playing the game, you may or may not come to agree that noise is intrusive on order, inimical to culture and to being human; that anti-art and mere galaxies of *signifiants* would be as fatal to our society as incest. But the ambiguous status of the riddles—and the whole book is one —must qualify the force of such conclusions. The speaking animal lives in nature by his power to create systems homologous with language. True or false? Lévi-Strauss himself describes as myths the transformations by which he illustrates this thesis. Burgess sees the point that books, like riddles, may best be left unanswered. And when you get through the apricot to the stone you find no hard organic substance, nothing unambiguous, but a riddle, a content at best dangerous and anyway problematical.

Here I am reminded of a lucid observation made by Barthes

nine years ago, before he developed his current method of analysis. "A work of literature," he said then, "or at least of the kind that is normally considered by the critics (and this itself may be a possible definition of 'good' literature) is neither ever quite meaningless (mysterious or 'inspired') nor ever quite clear; it is, so to speak, *suspended* meaning; it offers itself to the reader as a declared system of significance, but as a signified object it eludes his grasp. This kind of *dis-appointment* or *de-ception* . . . inherent in the meaning explains how it is that a work of literature has such power to ask questions of the world . . . without, however, supplying any answers." [17] Here we have the nub of the matter. Barthes's insight owes something to the *nouveau roman;* a consciousness that deception (in the French sense, "disappointment") was an inherent property of narratives made Robbe-Grillet design his novels to demonstrate it, and the necessity of *deception* to the modern novel is an important theme of *Pour un nouveau roman*. Robbe-Grillet himself allowed that what he was doing was revolutionary only if one made the mistake of assuming that the "rules" of the novel were established in Balzac's day. Barthes's developing mystique of *écriture* led him beyond this position; in 1963 he still, I think, had it right.

If he did, then of course it must be wrong to assume that a novel such as *MF*, for all its *lisibilité*, cannot exemplify "suspended meaning," pose questions and disappoint the answer, constitute a world in which everything is in *en jeu*, and in this way validate its relationship to a world elsewhere of which the

[17] Roland Barthes, "Criticism as Language," *Times Literary Supplement*, September 27, 1963, 739–40.

same may be said. The difference between *lisible* and *scriptible* cannot be stated as simply as Barthes came to think, perhaps need not have been stated at all.

Perhaps some readers may have been induced, by the foregoing, to think of a more familiar book—one that contrives, without explicit advertisement, to raise the question of suspended meaning and ask questions which cannot be answered by an appeal to some incontrovertible, unproblematic structure. In *The Crying of Lot 49*, Pynchon's Oedipa, as her name implies, is also confronted with riddles and with the obligation to discover an order. The origin of these riddles is in doubt; it may be the nature of the human world, viewable as waste or as system; it may be a man called Inverarity, who in turn may be either untruth or *dans le vrai*. The book is crammed with disappointed promises of significance, with ambiguous invitations to paradigmatic construction, and this is precisely Oedipa's problem. Is there a structure *au fond*, or only deceptive galaxies of signifiers? Like California itself, the text offers a choice: plenitude or vacuity. Is there a hidden plot concerning an almost Manichaean conflict, which makes sense, whether evil or benign, of the randomness of the world?

Consider the opening: we find Oedipa returning from a Tupperware party; I understand that on these occasions goods are sold outside the normal commercial system. She stands in her living-room before a blank television set (communication system without message) and considers the randomness she projects on the world: thoughts about God, a Mexican hotel, dawn at Cornell, a tune from Bartok, a Vivaldi concerto for kazoo. Soon we hear about the coded voices of Inverarity, the culinary jumble of a Southern Californian supermarket, her husband's life as a used-car salesman, systematizing, giving meaning to, the trash in old cars. Now he works on a pop radio station, the communication system—without content —of another culture. Later he will start *listening* to Muzak, another type of the empty system. In a world where the psychiatrists provide material for paranoid fantasies, and lawyers are locked in imaginary rivalries with Perry Mason, everybody is tending toward his own dissident universe of meaning; Oedipa is Rapunzel, her own reality let down like hair from her head. Minority cultures, bricolaged from pop, old movies, astrology, coexist in a world whose significances, if any, relate to no conceivable armature.

But Oedipa has "all manner of revelations," and a shadowy armature seems to be taking shape. Is she still in her head, or is the great plot real? If so, is it malign? To discover it may be the same thing as inventing it. What Peter Berger and Thomas Luckmann call "the social construction of reality" proceeds because there are phenomena we cannot simply wish away; death is one, but there are others. The construction is what our social situation permits—say, the national limits, the limits of California, ultimately the limits of dissident groups and our protestant selves. As we plot against reality we comply with or deviate from the institutionalized plots; a great deviation is called a sect if shared, paranoia if not. There is always a way of coding the material, even that which on other views is simply waste. Having instituted a system one keeps it intact either by legitimating extraneous material or, if that is too difficult, or the threat too great, by nihilating it.

Making sense of other somewhat arbitrary symbolic universes, understanding their construction, is an activity familiar to all critics. Certainly it involves choices, a limitation of pluralities. The activity of the critic, thus understood, is nomic. It seeks order, and is analogous to the social construction of reality. What Oedipa is doing is very like reading a book. Of course books can be read in very strange ways—a man once undertook to demonstrate infallibly to me that *Wuthering Heights* was an interlinear gloss on Genesis. How could this be disproved? He had hit on a code, and legitimated all the signs. Oedipa is afraid she may be like that man, or that she is drifting into paranoia, the normal hermeneutic activity in disease, and Pynchon's great subject.

She has contact with many sects: in advanced societies, such as Southern California, "socially segregated subuniverses of meaning," as Berger and Luckmann observe,[18] tend to multiply. When she sees a way of linking them together Oedipa is conscious of other terrors than paranoia. She dreads the anomic, the world collapsed into filth and randomness; but she also dreads an evil order. Pynchon invents the Scurvhamite sect, who abandoned a very mechanical double predestinarianism ("nothing ever happens by accident") for the consolations of single predestination to damnation. Yet even on her wild San Francisco night Oedipa doesn't unambiguously believe in the patterns to which the evidence is apparently pointing. For instance, she dismisses the evidence of the children's rhymes. The entire structure is *à la fois posé et déçu*. We do

[18] Peter L. Berger and Thomas Luckmann, *The Social Construction of Reality* (New York, 1967), p. 85.

not learn whether the dove, harmonizer of tongues, which would make all these meaning-systems mutually intelligible, descended with the auctioneer's hammer; *au fond*, the plot remains suspended.

What concerns us is precisely the existence of what seem to be systems that could transmit meanings, as in the account of San Narciso, the town which looks like a printed circuit, "an intent to communicate. There'd seemed no limit to what the printed circuit could have told her (if she had tried to find out); so, in her first minute of San Narciso, a revelation trembled, just past the threshold of meaning." The revelation would be of the kind that explains the whole of history, the present condition of America, Inverarity, Wharfinger's play, and so on; it woul explain how waste has meaning, just as, couched as an acronym, WASTE forms a sentence ("We await sad Tristero's empire"). But Oedipa is poised on the slash between meaning and unmeaning, as she is between smog and sun; interminably confronted with meaningless binary choices —artificial light in sunlight, the statue of the hooker/nymph, which is both still and windblown—and by repetitions of the San Narciso situation: windows and bottles emptily reflecting the sun, messageless. The need of a revelation, the sense that such systems exist to transmit sense, drives us to find meaning in them, for we feel "as if, on some other frequency . . . words were being spoken." This is the sense in which Professor Mendelson is right in emphasizing the pentecostal themes in the book; fifty may follow forty-nine, and if it were called we should all become competently polyglot, able to hear the words we think are being spoken but cannot quite hear.

This is why Oedipa continues her game of strip-Botticelli
with the world. Her trial run with Metzger—merely on the
plot of an old movie—sensitized her for a revelation; just as
the flight of the rogue aerosol foreshadows a world which,
though unpredictable, is determinate. And so she continues to
spot the clues, though never sure where they are, in her head
or out there. The text only says it is "as if . . . there were a
revelation in progress all round her." Options remain nag-
gingly open, as when the naval action of Peter Pinguid, that
ancestor of Inverarity, is described: "off the coast of what is
now Carmel-by-the-Sea, or what is now Pismo Beach, around
noon or possibly towards dusk, the two ships sighted each
other. One of them may have fired; if it did the other re-
sponded." This niggling dubiety is Oedipa's, and the text's.

The messages sent by the illicit system are normally without
content; this could be true of the novel. The clues pile up.
The Courier's Tragedy (played in a theater located between a
traffic-analysis firm and a wildcat transistor outfit, circulation
and communication) relates not only to the supposed history
of Tristero but to incest, tongueless attempts to pray, an anti-
Paraclete. The bones of the dead are turned into ink, a means
of empty communication (or into wine and cigarettes, which
belong to other systems). Ralph Driblette has heard a message
in the system of the play; so could Oedipa, if she gave herself
to it. Everything can be legitimated, systematized. But there
are only clues, "never," we are told, "the central truth itself,
for if that should blaze out it would destroy its own message
irreversibly." If the systems are to work, and the book to work
as a system, it will be because the reader can do what Oedipa

could not when confronted with Maxwell's demon: make the piston move, reverse the entropy of communication as that device reverses physical entropy. But if you make the eyes of this novel move, or if you believe in the original plot on which it depends, you risk a kind of madness, which is the ultimate human cost of holding everything together in a single design. The systems are there to be filled: children's rhymes, the "coded years of uselessness" in the mattresses of the poor, the societies of queers and failed suicides, all to be handled if you want a central truth, a word to reconcile your time with eternity. Nobody helps; Oedipa's friends drop away. The more she encodes the trash of America the more critical her isolation becomes. She is like the poor of whom she has heard, camping among telephone wires; she walks as if inside a digital computer, among either-ors, waiting for the systems to contain a message. Either there is a Tristero, or she is "orbiting in the ecstasy of a true paranoia."

We can't, of course, be told which, and we question the novel as Oedipa does the Tristero plot. That plot is pointed to as the object of some possible annunciation; but the power is in the pointing, not in any guarantee. One could talk for hours about this remarkable work, but at the bottom of all one said would be the truth that it imitates the texts of the world, and also imitates their problematical quality. If one coded *Lot 49*, its radical equivocations would be instantly evident—the cultural code, for example, is as little the inert congeries proposed by Barthes as the hermeneutic code is a progress to *dévoilement*. Its separation from its exterior and its totality are precisely what it is *about*. It is an invitation to the speaking animal to consider what he makes of the world into which he introduces his communication systems; and it asks him to read a text, to reread it, to produce it if that is a better word. In its totality it posses the choice: *plein/vide*, as it so often does in its texture. To seek an answer is to be disappointed, *déçu*. Deception is the discovery of the novel, not of its critics.

Needing sharp instances, I've chosen to write about two novels which refer more or less directly to a kind of world-plot prior to their own. But one could extend the argument to cover almost any book we think worth reading; the category of the *lisible* virtually melts away, since all such books assume that they will be competently read—"produced"—not, of course, because they are complex riddles, but because they know, as if by introspection, that it is a property of narratives (doubtless often neglected) to be plural, self-examining, incapable of full closure, as indeed the history of interpretation confirms.

Let me add one more brief example, of a novel quite different from those I have discussed—a text which exploits without advertising its suspension of meaning. It is Henry Green's *Loving*. Edward Stokes, in the best available study of this neglected writer,[19] says he finds the book difficult because it offers no interpretative hints. There are unmotivated rhetorical shifts, sudden switches of level. Sometimes it sounds like fairy tale, sometimes like proletarian realism. Still, says Mr. Stokes, Green must be talking about the disintegration of the class system, a theme he had handled in earlier novels. The de-

[19] Edward Stokes, *The Novels of Henry Green* (London, 1959).

caying Irish castle, with its selfish, empty gentry and its eva-
sive, quarreling, draft-dodging servants, must have something
to do with that theme. But why do patterns interfere with one
another as they do? Why, for instance, does the coarse, seedy
butler Raunce fall ecstatically in love with the implausibly
beautiful housemaid Edith and why does he go back to England and join the army?

True, there are symbols—the peacocks especially, and
their eggs; the doves; the weathervane stuck with its arrow
pointing to a scene of adultery because a live mouse is caught
in its cogs. Something might be made of all that. But "the difficulty," says Mr. Stokes, is that "there is no single, central,
all-important clue," and so "the symbols remain . . . free and
unassigned." (Why then are they symbols?) He cannot reduce
their "perpetual cross-flickering . . . to any simple statement
of meaning"; at best he can guess what some of them "imply
or insinuate." The story about the loves and marriages of the
doves, told by a nurse while before the very eyes of the children real doves mate and murder, is, says Mr. Stokes, more
hopefully, "a microcosm of the whole novel." [20] I think he was
wiser when in doubt that anything could make this claim. The
right reaction here is surely suspicion. The book is so shifty
—the dialogue is particularly surprising, for instance, especially if we recall that Green is the greatest English master of
working-class speech—should one not have doubts about so
neat a contraption? Elsewhere *Loving* flourishes its "symbols"
only as if to trick us. The peacocks are something to do with

[20] *Ibid.*, pp. 162, 163, 164.

lust, greed, and so on, but these equivalences are undermined. Green appears to be doing exactly as he pleases, with complete disregard for any desire we may have to extract the fruit stone. The game of blindman's buff among the statues, the girls dancing in the vast ballroom, they don't, except for the intrusions of Raunce, dyspeptic and venal, have much to do with anything else; or Paddy among the peacocks, or Mrs. Jack taken in adultery, or the lisping insurance man, or the housemaids innocently lesbian in their room, or the conventional plot about a missing ring. All the gestures and tones warn us that it is risky to take the dove-story as straight irony; and so does the narrative, for the maids arrive on the scene "in long purple uniforms, swaying towards them in soft sunlight through the budding branches, fingers on lips. . . . All began soundlessly giggling in the face of beauty."

The simple closure is frustrated; so is Mr. Stokes. In the concluding pages of the novel, after Raunce has decided to take Edith back to unsafe England, he lies, apparently ill, as peacocks extravagantly surround, and doves settle on his girl. "And their fluttering disturbed Raunce, who reopened his eyes. What he saw then he watched so that it could be guessed that he was in pain with his great delight. For what with the peacocks bowing at her purple skirts, the white doves nodding on her shoulders round her brilliant cheeks, and her great eyes that blinked tears of happiness, it made a picture." It would be profitable, were there time, to analyze this extraordinary passage in detail; perhaps it is obvious that anything so rhetorically devious is unlikely to be straightforward in other ways. Mr. Stokes thinks it leads directly to the conclusion, to

Raunce's return to England, home, and duty, and the pleasures of marriage. Certainly the text ends, a few words later, by saying that they returned to England and "lived happily ever after"; but it had opened thus: "Once upon a day an old butler . . . lay dying, "muttering the name of Ellen while Raunce stole his office and his whisky. Yet Raunce could be dying. If we are not seduced by a naïve desire for *dévoilement* we shall see that the text is not naïvely transparent. The evidence points in many ways, and Green simply allows it to do so. It invites structuration and strongly questions the notion of definitive structures. Without using the devices of the *nouveau roman*, it assumes that the problematical character of what may be *au fond* is a property of narrative; it accepts and exploits the pluralities that arise from this situation.

Once the problem of closure is stated in this more general way it becomes obvious that there is nothing new about suspending it. Think of James in *The Sacred Fount*, where it remains for ever uncertain whether there is anything at all *au fond*, or in "The Figure in the Carpet," a comic handling of the whole question, though it emerges that the forces which prevent the critic (the narrator and us) from discovering the figure are love and death, the very powers which make us want legitimated life-plots and closures.

MF has a problematical content which itself forms the envelope of more content, consisting of solutions, right or wrong, to mythical riddles. It displays randomness subjected to human intentions and ideas of order. That it enacts the arbitrariness, the chanciness, of such order—there are texts everywhere but not everything is a text—validates not the explanations of Lévi-Strauss but its own status as a characteristic product of *homo faber;* it is aware of its own chimerical nature. As for *Lot 49,* it indicates the enormous absurdity of both assumptions: that there is a structure, and that there is not. Neither book endorses any simple requirement of full closure. Each knows, like James, that between such desires in the reader and the actuality of the text there is a gap that is dangerous to the point of madness, and that the reader must be responsible for what he does with it. And it is in this light that we should reconsider the view that the *lisible* text is a *naïve* chimera.

Finally the codes again. In some modified form they have use in textual analysis. As they stand they depend on an untrustworthy historical theory and a perverse valuation of the *lisible,* which is represented as nauseous except insofar as it has the luck to anticipate a meaningless modernity, and which is anyway a category of straw. Probably the basic issue is between those who think that textual simulacra of order and system must be ideological (nauseous) and those who take them to be responses to a more radical need for satisfaction, a need which the anthropology of *la pensée sauvage,* and the sociology of knowledge, each in its different way, confirms.

The pluralities of sense available to *zoon phonanta* appear to be indeterminate but none the less systematically limited. That suggests that we can have a humanly adequate measure of plurality without abandoning all notions of structure, especially as structure is itself problematical. Perhaps we need once again to remind ourselves that the theory of infinite structuration is historically part of the continuing French reaction against an atavistic academic criticism. This has entailed the false assumption that flexible, productive, and plural reading is to be had only on the basis of new and revolutionary theoretical agreements. But these are circuitous routes to truths more readily accessible: the novel itself has long been aware of its chimerical potential; it is an authentic *faux-naïf*, expert in the limitations of its own pluralities. *That* self-consciousness, rather than an unwilling symbolic permissiveness, is what preserves the *lisible* as something more than an imperfect herald of the truly modern.

RICHARD OHMANN
Literature as Act

J INTEND THIS ESSAY as assistance to those—
almost all of us—not satisfied with taking literary
works to be structures, objects, artifacts. Literature plainly has,
also, a dynamic aspect. In order to conceptualize that side of
literature, I will turn to J. L. Austin's theory of speech acts for
basic ideas and three or four terms.

Austin combined interests in language and in the theory of
action. He pointed out that we can commonly describe a single event as several different acts, depending on how much we
take in of intention, planning, execution, consequence, and
context. We can conceive Lee Harvey Oswald's act as tensing
his forefinger, pulling a trigger, firing a gun, shooting Presi-
dent Kennedy, murdering him, or assassinating him. The sequence of descriptions represents a widening of our conception.

Similarly, in uttering a sentence, say "Batter my heart,
three-personed God," one performs acts on different levels,
three of which are of particular consequence for linguistic and
literary theory. The locutionary act (I will use Austin's fairly
cumbersome terms) is simply that of saying an English sentence with a particular meaning; that is, of producing the
sounds and structures that constitute that sentence. The illocu-

tionary act—that act performed in saying the sentence—
may be that of *demanding, requesting, imploring, praying;* [1]
its exact force remains uncertain without more context, but
clearly the speaker is trying with the power of his speech to
direct or bind the future conduct of his God.[2] The perlocutionary act—for example, pleasing, persuading, annoying
—is performed upon an interlocutor by or through the uttering of the sentence. To give a speech act its perlocutionary
description is to include more of its consequences. Perlocutionary acts are more unpredictable, because not inherent in the form of the sentence and the social situation alone.
A *prayer* may go astray, fall on deaf ears, stir mercy or venge-
fulness. It all depends.[3]

Grammar deals with the well-formedness of locutions, and
rhetoric with the effectiveness of perlocutions. For illocutions,
Austin called the analogous dimension "felicity." An illocu-

---

[1] I will italicize words for illocutionary acts throughout.

[2] His act belongs to an important class I call *Influencers*. In this
essay I will not try to maintain strict terminology. For a more
technical analysis of the various illocutions, see my "Instrumental
Style," in *Current Trends in Stylistics*, ed. Braj B. Kachru (Edmonton, 1972).

[3] Austin expounded the theory of speech acts in his posthumous
How to Do Things with Words (Cambridge, Mass., 1962). For
elaborations see John Searle, *Speech Acts* (Cambridge, 1969);
Charles J. Fillmore, "Verbs de jugement: Essai de description se-
mantique," *Langages*, V (1970), 56–72; Zeno Vendler, "Les per-
formatifs en perspective," *Langages*, V (1970), 73–90. Fillmore's
essay appears in English in *Studies in Linguistic Semantics*, ed.
Charles J. Fillmore and D. Terence Langendoen (New York,
1971).

tionary act is felicitous if (1) the participants are qualified and appropriate, (2) the circumstances are right, (3) the verbal formula is spoken accurately and completely, (4) the speaker's beliefs and feelings are those required for performance of the act in good faith, and (5) the participants conduct themselves appropriately afterwards. A teacher can terminate a class using one of many illocutions, the most formal of which is perhaps "I hereby dismiss the class." He is the right person to do so, and the verbal formula is available. If there is nothing in the circumstances that blocks the act, if the teacher has suitable feelings and beliefs, and if members of the class do in fact disband, that completes the illocutionary act of *dismissing* the class. What would make Donne's *prayer* felicitous is a more complicated question, but let us stick to easy cases.

In a play, the action rides on a train of illocutions. Not that locutionary content or perlocutionary effect are unimportant, or indeed separable from the illocutions. But movement of the characters and changes in their relations to one another within the social world of the play appear most clearly in their illocutionary acts.

MRS BAINES: I hope we shall have enough to keep all the shelters open. Lord Saxmundham has promised us five thousand pounds—
BARBARA: Hooray!
JENNY: Glory!
MRS BAINES: —if—
BARBARA: 'If!' If what?
MRS BAINES: —if five other gentlemen will give a thousand each to make it up to ten thousand.

BARBARA: Who is Lord Saxmundham? I never heard of him.

UNDERSHAFT: (*who has pricked up his ears at the peer's name, and is now watching Barbara curiously*) A new creation, my dear. You have heard of Sir Horace Bodger?

BARBARA: Bodger! Do you mean the distiller? Bodger's whisky!

UNDERSHAFT: That is the man. He is one of the greatest of our public benefactors. He restored the cathedral at Hakington. They made him a baronet for that. He gave half a million to the funds of his party: they made him a baron for that.

SHIRLEY: What will they give him for the five thousand?

UNDERSHAFT: There is nothing left to give him. So the five thousand, I should think, is to save his soul.

MRS BAINES: Heaven grant it may! Oh Mr Undershaft, you have some very rich friends. Cant you help us towards the other five thousand? We are going to hold a great meeting this afternoon at the Assembly Hall in the Mile End Road. If I could only announce that one gentleman had come forward to support Lord Saxmundham, others would follow. Dont you know somebody? couldnt you? wouldnt you? (*her eyes fill with tears*) oh, think of those poor people, Mr Undershaft: think of how much it means to them, and how little to a great man like you.

UNDERSHAFT: (*sardonically gallant*) Mrs Baines: you are irresistible. I cant disappoint you; and I cant deny myself the satisfaction of making Bodger pay up. You shall have your five thousand pounds.

MRS BAINES: Thank God!

UNDERSHAFT: You dont thank me?

MRS BAINES: Oh sir, dont try to be cynical: dont be ashamed

of being a good man. The Lord will bless you abundantly; and our prayers will be like a strong fortification round you all the days of your life. (*With a touch of caution*) You will let me have the cheque to shew at the meeting, wont you? Jenny: go in and fetch a pen and ink. (*Jenny runs to the shelter door*).

UNDERSHAFT: Do not disturb Miss Hill: I have a fountain pen (*Jenny halts. He sits at the table and writes the cheque. Cusins rises to make room for him. They all watch him silently*).

BILL: (*cynically, aside to Barbara, his voice and accent horribly debased*) Wot prawce selvytion nah?

BARBARA: Stop. (*Undershaft stops writing: they all turn to her in surprise*). Mrs Baines: are you really going to take this money?

(Act II; Penguin edition, pp. 105–7)

The scene that traces Major Barbara's disillusionment with the Salvation Army, and ends in her resignation from it, first takes this direction with the announcement of a *promise*. Mrs. Baines, Barbara's commander, says that Lord Saxmundham will give the Army £5000 if five other gentlemen give a thousand each. There are many conditions for *promising* happily; the one essential to this action is that the future act to which the speaker binds himself be desired by those to whom it will be directed. You cannot felicitously *promise* to thrash me; that is a threat, and to use the word "promise" in making it is to speak figuratively.

Barbara initially *welcomes* the promised gift, with her "Hooray." But she reveals, in her next act, a *question*, that she has not taken in all the circumstances that surround the *promise*,

including one that will be critical for her in assessing its felicity: "Who is Lord Saxmundham? I never heard of him." Sir
Horace Bodger, Undershaft *tells* her. "Bodger! Do you mean
the distiller? Bodger's whisky!" A condition for felicitous
questioning is that the asker need or want the information, and
in the midst of a pragmatic conversation like the one at hand
this condition is tightened, I think: the inquiry must in some
way advance consideration of the issue. Clearly it does for Barbara. The promiser's moral character and intentions bear on
the felicity of his *promise*, and in fact determine whether she
would be party to it—agree to accept the gift and so bring
the promise to completion. As clearly, for Mrs. Baines this is
irrelevant. What emerges here is that the two women inhabit
worlds of value and convention that are different at least in
this one respect. People in a society share broadly the conventions for felicitous speech acts, but there is some variation—
understandably, since the rules are a kind of social contract,
based in ethics and even politics.

Undershaft, who sees the disagreement opening up between
Barbara and Mrs. Baines, widens it with his illocutions. Yes,
Bodger is the man. "He is one of the greatest of our public
benefactors." This is a *verdictive*, an act of *rating* a person,
act, thing, or whatever on some scale. For the verdictive to
work, the scale of worth itself must be granted prior validity
by the participants. Undershaft chooses his scale carefully: as
he goes on to explain the *rating*, Bodger "restored the cathedral at Hakington. They made him a baronet for that. He gave
half a million to the funds of his party: they made him a baron
for that." Undershaft means his act to pass muster with those

who think charity a social good even when done in self-interest. Mrs. Baines does, Barbara does not; Undershaft is detaching Barbara from the miniature society of the Army shelter by showing her that she does not really subscribe to its ethics. The dramatic irony here rests precisely in the ambivalence of Undershaft's act—felicitous for Mrs. Baines and seemingly, but not really, for him; infelicitous for Barbara and the audience. Besides, his act has a third force on another level. Undershaft's values are neither Barbara's nor Mrs. Baines's; for him public benefaction is in itself an evil. His *verdictive* implied endorsement of a scale he rejects, and so could not have been felicitous no matter what his audience's values.

When he next speaks, Undershaft drives the wedge of his irony in deeper: "There is nothing left to give him. So the five thousand, I should think, is to save his soul." This *conjecture* cannot be felicitous except in a company who believe that cold-blooded charity might in fact save the giver's soul. One cannot *conjecture* the impossible. Though Barbara is silent, we know that she is excluded from this company—she has insisted earlier that "the Army is not to be bought." So when Mrs. Baines seeks to validate Undershaft's preposterous act with a *prayer* of her own—"Heaven grant it may!"—the social cohesion of the Army officers has quite come apart. Barbara could no more entertain the felicity of such a *prayer* than could Undershaft, though for different reasons.

Now the plot moves forward quickly on rather formal illocutions. Mrs. Baines *requests* help from Undershaft in matching the five thousand. She *pleads*. He *agrees* to supply the money himself. She *thanks* God. These illocutions add up to a

new social compact, between the Salvation Army and the mu-
nitions maker. That this compact must exclude Barbara becomes inevitable in the next exchange. When Mrs. Baines
thanks God for the gift, Undershaft chides her, "You don't
thank *me?*" She responds with an act that is somewhere between *command* and *advice:* "Oh sir, don't try to be cynical:
don't be ashamed of being a good man." For the act to be felicitous, Mrs. Baines must have authority over Undershaft, as
well as moral superiority, he must accept this relative position,
and he must in fact have been "ashamed of being a good man,"
among other conditions. These conditions are so far from
being met that Mrs. Baines's attempting the act can only show,
to Barbara and the audience, how narrow is the moral universe
within which Mrs. Baines exercises her mission. Then she ce-
ments the absurdity by adding, "The Lord will bless you
abundantly; and our prayers will be like a strong fortification
round you all the days of your life." This attempt to fortify
the "prince of darkness" with *prayer* has to be either hypoc-
risy or intolerable innocence.

    As Undershaft is about to sign his check, Barbara breaks her
silence with a *command* to stop. This act, with the *challenge*
that follows—"Mrs. Baines: are you really going to take this
money?"—is Barbara's attempt to seize authority from the
new coalition that has been forming, and indeed to restore the
old lines of value and power, more in accord with her idealis-
tic image of the world. But it is too late for salvage. The argument that follows merely makes explicit the social division and
realignment that has already developed through less discursive
acts. Barbara is disenchanted; she no longer accepts the moral

authority of the Army, and when Mrs. Baines orders her to carry the flag on a march of celebration, Barbara defeats the act with a refusal—"I can't come." This is in effect her *resignation* from the Army, confirmed a bit later when she says she can't *pray*—can't, that is, felicitously perform an act that presupposes the Army's theology.

Illocutions are the vehicle of the play's action. There is a tendency to think of plays as moving the characters to new understandings, new "positions." This happens, to be sure, but it is the way of happening that is critical. As Barbara changes her position the movement is not only, and not even mainly, cognitive. An intricate conflict unfolds through the illocutions. Each speaker tries to act felicitously on his or her sense of appropriate social roles, relations of power, moral value, and metaphysical truth. Felicitous action would need these kinds of consonance. Failing consonance, speakers' acts are blocked, aborted, or in some way deprived of completion. Their failure in turn reveals the dissonance in ideas or values. Thus conflict is enacted, not in an idealized clash of positions or beliefs, whatever that would be. Illocutionary acts move the play along.

Plays and other literary forms relying on dialogue are particularly well suited to social themes. As speakers try to envelop one another in their worlds by winning acquiescence to the premises behind their illocutionary acts, conventions and decorums are thrown into action, and different models of the good society come into conflict. Shaw exploits the resonance of illocutions. They carry the audience of *Major Barbara* through successively more enlightened visions—that of Lady Britomart's home, Cusins's rationalism, Barbara'a salvationist ideal, Undershaft's combination of *realpolitik* and vitalism. Shaw's didactic intent and his dramaturgy blend more seamlessly than critics think who are in the habit of waiting for the big, discursive illocutions that supposedly unpack the meaning of the play.

Dialogue can also work economically to juxtapose different realities, and for the same reason. An illocutionary act that works within one reality is void in another. This shows most plainly when the speaker is not who he seems to be, when he pretends or comes in disguise. In *The Importance of Being Earnest*, Algernon intrudes, posing as the wayward Ernest, upon Jack's country retreat: "Brother John, I have come down to tell you that I am very sorry for all the trouble I have given you, and that I intend to lead a better life in the future." His ceremonial *greeting* to "Brother John," his *apology* for his nonexistent dissipations, and his *resolve* to lead a better life are all infelicitous because Algernon is not the appropriate person to enact them. Jack knows that, as does Algernon, but Cecily does not, since Jack has so carefully prepared the alternate world in which "Ernest" is a shameful reality. Hence she objects when Jack refuses to complete even the *greeting*, for that act should encounter no impedence in the reality she accepts.

This kind of thing is shallow enough, but the same principle is at work, more profoundly, when King Lear ceremonially measures out his lands in geometric correspondence to his daughters' professions of love. The terrible infelicity of his acts corresponds to the depth of his error about what sort of human reality an old king inhabits.

As illocutions erect competing realities through the action of a work, so illocutions gradually define the mode of reality that governs the whole work. To stick to the drama, one characteristic of both the high mimetic and, especially, the low mimetic modes is that consecutive illocutions, however they may clash in argument (that is, in "substance"), are strung on a taut thread of continuity. The participants dwell sufficiently in the same sort of reality that they can join their acts in pursuit of a common end. Consider this from Arthur Miller's *The Crucible:*

a PUTNAM: I do not think I saw you at Sabbath meeting since snow flew.

b PROCTOR: I have trouble enough without I come five mile to hear him preach only hell-fire and bloody damnation. Take it to heart, Mr. Parris. There are many others who stay

c away from church these days because you hardly ever mention God any more.

d PARRIS: (*Now aroused.*) Why, that's a drastic charge!

e REBECCA: It's somewhat true; there are many that quail to

f bring their children—

g PARRIS: I do not preach for children, Rebecca. It is not the

h children who are unmindful of their obligations toward this ministry.

i REBECCA: Are there really those unmindful?
PARRIS: I should say the better half of Salem village—
PUTNAM: And more than that!

The dispute begins with Putnam's *accusation* (a) of Proctor, plain enough in its illocutionary force, though not made explicit with an "I accuse. . . ." Proctor tries to blunt that force with a *justification* (b), then modulates into a *counter-accusation* (c) put directly to Parris: the minister never mentions God. Parris's response is a *verdictive* (d), recognizing the charge and *rating* (d) it as "drastic." Rebecca counters with another *verdictive* (e) and a different *rating* (e), and then with a further *charge* (f). Parris *rejects* (g) a presupposition of that charge—that he should be preaching for children—then *justifies* (h) the severity of his preaching by means of a further *charge* (h), which Rebecca *challenges* (i), and so on. Although the exchange is heated and the speakers at odds, all of them accept the tacit agenda, the validity of the project (establishing blame and moral credit), the likelihood of advancing it through talk, and major values like that of Christian piety. Building from so shared a world, the dialogue can proceed to adjudicate matters of fact, of the precise moral weighting of past acts, of character and worth. The illocutionary milieu is pragmatic and cooperative. Would it be too much to suggest that a low mimetic tragedy is one whose characters fall short of the necessary skill in solving their problems? And that illocutionary exchanges are the chief means of problem-solving?

In the ironic mode this continuity tends to dissipate. It represents a measure of social cohesion, after all, and reflects the participants' joint conviction that they have at least some power to deal rationally with their troubles. The hopelessness of a play like Samuel Beckett's *Endgame* derives partly from the social incoherence within which its people talk.

HAMM: The dog's gone.
CLOV: He's not a real dog, he can't go.

HAMM: (*groping*) He's not there.

CLOV: He's lain down.

HAMM: Give him up to me. (*Clov picks up the dog and gives it to Hamm. Hamm holds it in his arms. Pause. Hamm throws away the dog.*) Dirty brute! (*Clov begins to pick up the objects lying on the ground.*) What are you doing?

CLOV: Putting things in order. (*He straightens up. Fervently.*) I'm going to clear everything away! (*He starts picking up again.*)

HAMM: Order!

CLOV: (*straightening up*) I'm doing my best to create a little order.

HAMM: Drop it! (*Clov drops the objects he has picked up.*)

CLOV: After all, there or elsewhere. (*He goes towards door.*)

HAMM: (*irritably*) What's wrong with your feet?

CLOV: My feet?

HAMM: Tramp! Tramp!

CLOV: I must have put on my boots.

HAMM: Your slippers were hurting you? (*Pause.*)

CLOV: I'll leave you.

HAMM: No!

CLOV: What is there to keep me here?

HAMM: The dialogue.

There are constant difficulties of sequence. Hamm fails to follow up on his *request* for the dog; a requester must want the thing he *requests*, and conduct himself accordingly afterward. Clov deserts the issue of the dog, and begins his cleanup; *challenged*, he builds an ecstatic *justification*, but Hamm *questions* him a third time as if he had never spoken. Clov's act has fallen into a void of a sort doubtless more common at home than on the stage. Clov's third *explanation* is the same as his others, and as ineffectual in bringing Hamm into some relation with the topic of order. Hamm's command, "Drop it," is surprisingly felicitous, though, and Clov abruptly abandons his project. As he does so he denies its premise, his supposed love of order, and so renders his earlier explanation unhappy. Similarly short-lived are the topics of Clov's feet and his determination to leave Hamm. These speakers cannot hold together for more than moments any fixity of utilitarian purpose, or even the minimum sharing of presuppositions that makes a speech community possible.

Illocutionary action is action on a social plane. It relies for success on those things that make up a society: for instance, definitions of role and relation, stable distribution of power, conventions of intimacy and distance, manners. Where these bonds are shattered or nebulous, illocutionary action becomes awkward or impossible. Much contemporary literature has seized on the fascination of such a disorder, not just absurd theater, but fiction, the Beatles, the far-out television commercials.

By commenting on a few passages from plays, I have meant to give some substance to the more theoretical claims I now turn to. They concern, in the first place, the ontology of literary works.

"A poem is made out of words." Critics who quote this remark often do so with an air of hailing fanciful and vagrant theorists back to the simple truth. A critical era might be measured by the truths it takes to be simple, obvious, and fundamental. Thus an ontology of literature that finds rock bottom in words lends itself well to practical criticism that searches

out the structures in a poem or novel or play and tries to identify the unique meaning of those structures—criticism that
conceives the poem as an artifact. It is easy to suppose that the
poet takes words out of the language, joins them together, and
lets them loose in the world, where they forever carry their
complex of feelings, images, and ideas, releasing it when
tapped by a reader of ideal temperament and wit. I think that
these are common presuppositions of the past forty years or so.

Well, isn't literature made of words? There is a stone for Dr.
Johnson to kick at, surely. The revisionist impulse contained in
my title does not extend to proving the words illusory, or
showing that there is a rock bottom even rockier than they.
Poems are made of words, but the danger in taking much
comfort from this reassurance is in forgetting how many other
"things" poems are "made of." Not just sounds, phrases, sentences, but more evanescent parts like structures, meanings,
feelings, ideas, patterns, images. Perhaps even a short list like
this suffices to call in question the aptness of the metaphor
"made of" as more than a handy but casual way to refer to the
insides of literary works. The idea of composing discourses is
not a post-Gutenberg invention. But I don't doubt that use of
print has made it seem natural to think of discourses as compo-
sitions, and to analyze them into "parts."

Whatever the encouragement we may get from Gutenberg
or Ramus, certainly the conceptual models of literature that
we have kept readiest to hand have been static models. Metaphors like "urn" and "icon" seem appropriate. We see the
poem as an artifact, and chart its structure. If it contains dynamic impulses, they are held in a tension that neutralizes
them; I. A. Richards spoke of poetry's checking the impulse to

action by balancing our "appetencies." W. K. Wimsatt said that the poem is an act, but that it must be hypostatized as "a thing between the poet and the audience," before it becomes available for criticism. And of course a brilliant criticism has issued from these premises—in fact more than one kind of criticism, for New Criticism has its parallel in most of the criticism, like Roman Jakobson's, sponsored by formal linguistics. The parallel makes sense, because linguistics has generally adopted the same methodological strategy Wimsatt spoke of, and treated discourse as text, rather than act. But that is another story.

Some critics have been uneasy with this arrangement. Kenneth Burke developed a theory of poetry as symbolic action. But he left the weight heavily on "symbolic." The poem was a surrogate act in the drama of self, an instrument of purgation or redemption. You might say it was what the poet did instead of "really" doing something. Similarly, R. P. Blackmur could not much refine his perception that words are "made of action or response," because he let it drift into impressionism and mystery. More recently Richard Poirier has attacked the "packaging" of literature as a corpus of finished works for classroom analysis. Poirier would have us respond instead to the power, "still generating in those works, of the retraceable acts of writing, composition, performance," and participate with our own energies in literature's struggle, its "wrestling with words and meaning." [4] This is a version of literature, and

[4] "What Is English Studies, and If You Know What That Is, What Is English Literature?" in *The Performing Self* (New York, 1971), p. 84.

the teaching of literature, that would be attractive to many, myself included. But it is hard to derive from the assumption on which most teachers of literature have built their criticism, namely, that the poem is a thing made of words. To help us get beyond exhortation and resolve, in thinking of literature as act, we need a boost from theory.

As indicated above, I think that Austin's analysis is a useful footing. It shows that, in a quite literal way, the poem is made of acts. But it needs adaptation to the subject of literature, for I have been blinking a large difficulty: to wit, although within the dramatic worlds I have discussed, some illocutions are felicitous and some not, plainly when we refer these acts to their real participants—author, actors, audiences—*none* of them is, or could be, felicitous. Shaw doesn't perform the *promises*, *ratings*, *refusals*, etc., that make up his play, nor do his actors. Nor do the acts come at and involve audiences as *promises*, *ratings*, and *refusals* do outside the theater. A play is a play, and its verbal acts are of a different logical order from those of talk. Literary works are discourses with the usual illocutionary rules suspended, acts without consequences of the usual sort.[5] Jean-Paul Sartre is one who marks this sharp division— between poetry and prose, as he has it. The poet takes the act out of words: "One might think that he is composing a sentence but this is only what it appears to be. He is creating an object."[6] This last sentence seems perverse, though under-

[5] I made this argument at length in "Speech Acts and the Definition of Literature," *Philosophy and Rhetoric*, IV (1971), 1–19.

[6] Jean-Paul Sartre, *What Is Literature?* tr. Bernard Frechtman (New York, 1966), p. 8.

standable. An act dislodged from immediate practical ends may seem like no act at all. But that is too quick a move.

When a playwright gives written utterance to a declarative sentence, he is not, to be sure, stating it. What he does is something like putting words in another's mouth. Yet the "other" does not really exist. More precisely, the writer puts out imitation speech acts *as if* they were being performed by someone. Since that someone has no prior existence, in effect he is largely created by the assignment of speech acts. We ordinarily think of the playwright as creating characters and assigning lines to them, but it is the other way around: assigning lines is the means of creating characters, along with gesture, costume, motion. Similarly, a novelist creates his narrator and a poet his persona by the assignment of illocutions.

Let us examine this process from the reader's standpoint. He receives a series of illocutions divorced from their actual originator. Though what he knows of the poet—if anything —may influence him, in the paradigm case he has nothing to guide his understanding except the purported speech acts of one or more personae. From these he makes inferences of many kinds: who the speaker is, what roles he plays, what kind of society he lives in, whether he is reliable, what relationship he intends to establish between himself and his interlocutor, and so on. The reader makes these judgments in large part by putting to work his tacit knowledge of the conditions for happily performing illocutionary acts. If a poem begins "Batter my heart, three-personed God," the reader is forced into hypotheses about the kind of speaker who might properly issue this *plea*, about what beliefs and feelings it commits him to, about the degree of his good faith, about the conventions for verbal action in his world, and so on. In short, the reader builds on his tacit knowledge of the conventions—past and present, actual and possible—for illocutionary acts, and what he builds is an image of the world implied by the acts that constitute the work.[7] This fairly complicated transaction between writer and reader is, I believe, what we can legitimately mean by "mimesis" in literary works.

Certainly the matter is more complicated than even a good Freudian critic like Norman Holland suggests, though I like his attempt, in *The Dynamics of Literary Response*, to analyze what actually happens in the commerce between work and reader. Holland says that the reader "introjects the literary work so that what happens 'in' it feels as though it were happening 'in' him." [8] Then the reader's capacity for fantasy and the work's potential interact, with the outcome being a pleasurable containment, in literary form and acceptable meaning, of the more dangerous fantasy material. My objection to this is that Holland takes the work to be "a discrete collection of words," and that accordingly the word "introject" slurs over a subtle transaction. Since what Holland leaves out is mainly the social content of the transaction, it is natural that his analysis of literary response should emphasize universals of the individual psyche, more than I think warranted. Mimesis draws into play the reader's social self.

In effect, mimesis reverses the usual direction of inference.

[7] See J. L. Styan's chapter on "Audience Participation," in *The Elements of Drama* (Cambridge, 1969), pp. 231–55. See also my "Speech, Literature, and the Space Between," *New Literary History*, IV (1972–73), 47–63.

[8] New York, Oxford University Press, 1968, p. 179.

As we participate in speech, we use what we know of the speaker and of circumstances to determine the felicity of the illocutions. In mimesis we assume felicity and infer a speaker and a fictional world from the circumstances that felicity requires. Needless to add, we may drop the hypothesis of felicity at any time, given conflicts within the work or between the work and what we know of the world.

I have no space to exemplify this in detail, but those who have read Stanley Fish's *Surprised by Sin* may regard large parts of his argument as illustrative. Fish shows, in my terms, that Milton throws unusual obstacles in the path of the reader participating in the mimesis of *Paradise Lost*. The poem allows competing hypotheses about the felicity of various acts, particularly the narrator's. Thus one issue between Fish and A. J. A. Waldock is precisely whether the narrator—and through him Milton—speaks felicitously in commenting on Satan's first address:

> So spake th'Apostate Angel, though in pain,
> Vaunting aloud, but tackt with deep despair.

Waldock thinks Milton has made Satan's speech obviously felicitous, and cannot take back that felicity with the *verdictives* carried by "vaunting" and "despair." The narrator's "allegation" can have no authority comparable to the foregoing "demonstration" (Waldock is using a rough-and-ready language of illocutions here). Fish sees the narrator's comments as challenging and finally overthrowing the reader's first, and defective, participation in the mimetic process. By making the reader relinquish, again and again, his first approximations of a felicitous response, Milton challenges his presuppositions, makes him recognize his own defective moral instincts, and rectifies his faith. At least so it may happen, Fish says, with readers less refractory than Waldock and Empson.[9]

A written literary work preserves in its words a record of purported speech acts. They are frozen in its text, to be brought alive whenever a reader reenacts them as a participant. I think that Fish is right in suggesting that the stage of a literary work is the reader's mind, and in assigning the reader so active a role in mimesis. I would add that the action on the stage is illocutionary. Like illocutionary action outside literature, it is inescapably ethical.

Even the simplest lyric draws the reader into ethical interaction. Take Yeats's "The Coming of Wisdom with Time":

Though leaves are many, the root is one;
Through all the lying days of my youth
I swayed my leaves and flowers in the sun;
Now I may wither into the truth.

The title, of course, contains a *verdictive* (pronounced on the rest of the poem) whose felicity must be judged. But further, the reader must posit an aging speaker who applies the analogy of the tree to human life (is this felicitous?), who voices this *criticism* of his anarchic youth and the *wish* or *resolve* to wither into truth. Since there is no way to construct a character or history for the speaker outside the immediate act by

[9] Stanley Eugene Fish, *Surprised by Sin: The Reader in Paradise Lost* (New York, 1967), p. 5. Fish quotes from Waldock's *Paradise Lost and Its Critics*.

which he attempts to accommodate old age, the reader cannot measure the felicity of the act against other conduct of the speaker. In particular, he cannot sensibly wonder whether the speaker has feelings and beliefs appropriate to his act. So the reader can best judge the act by generalizing it, testing it against the condition of all old men. Could an old man console himself in this way? Is it proper to do so? Finally, participation in the acts of the poem will lead to questions like these, which always reach into the area of moral choice.

Not a surprising conclusion, to be sure. Many critics, of whom Yvor Winters is only the most insistent, have seen poems as moral judgments, and to that intuition I mean only to have added a sketch of *how* ethics are drawn into enactment of a poem. But I also think that the perspective of these remarks warrants going beyond the bald claim that reading literature is an ethical activity. Often enough, humanists who share that belief would make the ethics of literature either abstract and timeless, or purely personal, existential. This cannot be. At the base of all illocutions is a society. The rules for felicity, like the rules of grammar, are culture-specific; they regulate intercourse within a particular society. Literary mimesis implicates the reader in an imagined society by making him party to the acts that imply it. There is no ethically neutral way for him to fulfill this role. He must give consent to the ethos of the created society, or reserve his endorsement to one degree or another. Either way, the poem calls his political imagination into play, presses him into political choice.

This is easy to see in a polemical piece like "S. O. P.," from the anthology of poems by Vietnam veterans, *Winning Hearts and Minds*.[10]

> To build a "gook stretcher," all you need is:
> Two helicopters
> Two long, strong ropes,
> And one elastic gook.
>
> —Larry Rottmann

A reader's relationship to the poem is political not mainly because Vietnam is a "controversial" subject (think of all the war poetry that drains the controversy from its subject, eternalizes war), but because the reader must choose how to participate in the speech act, and decide in what way, if at all, it is felicitous. The act is that of *instructing*, the tone that of a manual. Now you can felicitously instruct someone in a skill only if the skill is in itself morally acceptable—otherwise you would be sanctioning immoral behavior, or tempting your interlocutor to it, not simply offering him a neutral means to an end. So the poem invites the reader to build and accept a social system in which torture is routinely approved—in fact, standard operating procedure—at least during a war. The poet, of course, expects the reader to withhold completion of this act; so the poem's irony works. But there is no evading the political and moral choice. The reader must complete the act or refuse, accept or reject the mundaneness of torture.

From an American reader, in 1973, the poem calls up a fur-

[10] Ed. Larry Rottmann, Jan Barry, and Basil T. Paquet (Brooklyn, 1972).

ther political response. It urges that to withdraw from the implied society of the fictional speech act entails withdrawing from the American social contract, at least insofar as it includes the Vietnam war and the stretching of "gooks." Anyone can imagine a variety of tactics that a variety of readers might use to negotiate this predicament. But I doubt that any of the strategies is nonpolitical. In my opinion the same is true of Yeats's poem, and all others, though normally the political choices required by the poem engage less directly with those we face outside the poem.

In a recent thoughtful book on political poetry, *Imagination and Power*, Thomas Edwards argues that a successful "public poem" depends on the perception that we are permitted no simple choice between what is private and what is public, that politics extends into all corners of our lives. Edwards is not himself sure that the perception is accurate, or that he can accept Gottfried Keller's aphorism, "everything is politics." [11] I think a strong case can be made, from the nature of speech and action, that in literature everything is indeed politics, so long as we resist the unwarranted inference that literature comprises nothing *but* politics.

I also think it follows from my argument that the participation of readers in mimesis will properly differ. Each reader has a gender, a class, a race, an age, an income, a personal and social past. Such things add up to a politics. It will not do to say, "Well enough, but the reader should work to transcend these particularities, since they limit his or her experience of the

[11] Thomas R. Edwards, *Imagination and Power: A Study of Poetry on Public Themes* (New York, 1971), pp. 224–25.

poem." If literature and mimesis work the way I have claimed, transcendence of politics exacts too great a price. *The Reader* [12] who figures so large in most criticism and teaching is someone who, while reading, denies his or her experience and being-in-the-world. The attempt to build a "world elsewhere," as Poirier argued in another of his books, cannot succeed. To hope that it can, to seek in literature a domain exempt from abrasion against our own contingencies, is not only to amputate a good part of ourselves but to reject the poem the poet wrote and the social foundations of speech itself. Almost everyone would agree that the ideal reader is an unattainable fiction. I think that effort spent in trying to approximate such a reader is effort misspent.

Three instances. Winters was right in stressing the ethics of literature, but his failure to understand its politics led to the ludicrous spectacle of his handing down his own peculiar biases, not as politically based preferences to be argued out politically, but as objective judgments to be accepted by all whose sensibilities were adequately developed. Second, although I admire Fish's bringing into focus readers' engagement with *Paradise Lost*, I think his way of conceiving The Reader —"we"—is often misleading. For example, he says that at the end of the poem "we descend from this imaginative height, from this total and self-annihilating union with the Divine, to re-enter the race of time. . . . The shattered visage of truth has been put back together in the experience of the poem, indeed

[12] For a good account of Everyteacher and Everystudent, and other ideal readers, see Brent Harold, "Beyond Student-Centered Teaching," *College English*, XXXIV (1972–73), 200–12.

by the experience of the poem, which, with our co-operation, has slowly (and sometimes deviously) purged our intellectual ray so that it is once more proportionable to truth the object of it." [13] As Tonto replied to the Lone Ranger when beset by hostile Indians, "What do you mean 'we,' white man?" Fish's use of "we" and "our," and of phrases like "this total and self-annihilating union with the Divine" and "the experience of the poem" which strip the experiencer of particularity and imply that union with the Divine is a proper response for any reader—critical usages like these are perhaps conveniences, but they unnaturally suppress truths about real readers.

My third instance: analyzing *Lady Chatterley's Lover*, Wayne Booth rightly says that Lawrence's having *dramatized* his ethic of warmhearted fucking by letting Mellors be its spokesman does not save the novel for those who (like Booth) cannot accept that ethic as admirable. "Those of us who reject this side of the book do so finally," he says, "on the grounds that what Mellors says implies for us a version of D. H. Lawrence that we cannot admire." [14] Some of us, maybe, but for most of the women students in my class last year the book was objectionable in a more immediate way. They said that to participate in the mimetic re-creation of Connie Chatterley as Lawrence saw her was for them impossible without self-betrayal. Clearly the book was a measurably different experience for the men and the women. Should we attribute this to lack of critical sophistication, and ask the students to grow out of these differences?

[13] Fish, *Surprised by Sin*, pp. 330–31.
[14] Wayne Booth, *The Rhetoric of Fiction* (Chicago, 1961), p. 80.

Literature is made of acts. Literature is political, for writers and readers. If these propositions hold up, they weigh most heavily not in the discourse of critics with one another but in the critics' work as teachers, and in our relations to mass culture. Louis Kampf and Paul Lauter write, in their introduction to *The Politics of Literature,* "It may seem a hard prescription to propose that teachers of literature, trained by graduate school in detachment and privacy, should conceive as central to their *work* entering actively into political struggle," but not if we agree that "what's at stake is . . . a life process in which books do shape what we see or hope for or do." [15] The rootedness of literature in speech acts gives their position theoretical strength.

[15] Louis Kampf and Paul Lauter, eds., *The Politics of Literature* (New York, 1972), p. 44.

STANLEY E. FISH

What Is Stylistics and Why Are They Saying Such Terrible Things About It?

THE FIRST OF the questions in my title—what is stylistics?—has already been answered by the practitioners of the art. Stylistics was born of a reaction to the subjectivity and imprecision of literary studies. For the appreciative raptures of the impressionistic critic, stylisticians purport to substitute precise and rigorous linguistic descriptions, and to proceed from those descriptions to interpretations for which they can claim a measure of objectivity. Stylistics, in short, is an attempt to put criticism on a scientific basis. Answering my second question—why are they saying such terrible things about it?—will be the business of this essay, and I would like to begin (somewhat obliquely, I admit) by quoting from the *New York Times Book Review* of April 23, 1972. On pages 18 and 19 of that issue we find the publishing firm of Peter Wyden, Inc., proclaiming the merits of a new book by Tom Chetwynd. The book is entitled *How to Interpret Your Own Dreams (In One Minute or Less)*. The title appears on a reproduction of the book jacket and beneath it are the following descriptive claims: "Your key to 583 Dream Subjects with 1442 Interpretations," "An Encyclopedic Dictionary." These claims are supported and extended by a report of the author's researches and by a portion of the index. "What do *you* dream about?" the reader is asked, "Angels (see page 171), Babies (page 150), Bells (page 40), Cars, Collisions, Cooking, Death, Dogs, Doors, Exams, Falling, Hands, Hats, Illness, Monsters, Mother, Nudity, Sex, Teeth, Travel . . ." "And these," the blurb continues, "are just a few of the 583 dream subjects covered." "To compile this book," we are told, "the author spent 10 years analyzing the works of Freud, Jung, Adler and other dream authorities. Carefully indexed and cross indexed, each dream subject is rated in four ways: what it most likely means; what it could well mean; what it might mean; and what it might possibly mean. . . . This remarkable dream dictionary enables you to look up any dream instantly . . . find complete clues to its meaning." Finally, and with typographic aids, the claims underlying these claims are put forward: in italics, *it really works*, and in large white letters against a black bar background, BASED ON SOLID SCIENCE.

However amusing one finds this advertisement, it would be a mistake to underestimate the desire to which it appeals: the desire for an instant and automatic interpretive procedure based on an inventory of fixed relationships between observable data and meanings, meanings which do not vary with context and which can be read out independently of the analyst or observer who need only perform the operations specified by the "key." It is a desire as new as information theory and as old as the impulse to escape from the flux and variability of the human situation to the security and stability of a timeless formalism. It is also, I think, the desire behind stylistics, and in the first part of this paper I should like to examine some representative attempts to achieve it.

My first example is taken from the work of Louis Milic, author of *A Quantitative Approach to the Style of Jonathan Swift* and other statistical and computer studies. In an article written for *The Computer & Literary Style*, Milic attempts to isolate the distinctive features of Swift's style.[1] He is particularly interested in the Swiftian habit of piling up words in series and in Swift's preference for certain kinds of connectives. His method is to compare Swift, in these and other respects, with Macauley, Addison, Gibbon, and Johnson, and the results of his researches are presented in the form of tables: "Word-Class Frequency Distribution of All the Whole Samples of Swift, with Computed Arithmetic Mean," "Percentage of Initial Connectives in 2000-Sentence Samples of Addison, Johnson, Macauley, and Swift," "Total Introductory Connectives and Total Introductory Determiners as Percentages of All Introductory Elements," "Frequency of Occurrence of the Most Common Single Three-Word Pattern as a Percentage of Total Patterns," "Total Number of Different Patterns per Sample." It will not be my concern here to scrutinize the data-gathering methods of Milic or the other stylisticians (although some of them are challengeable even on their own terms), for my interest is primarily in what is done with the data after they have been gathered. This is also Milic's interest, and in the final paragraphs of his essay he poses the major question: "What in-

[1] "Unconscious Ordering in the Prose of Swift," in *The Computer & Literary Style*, ed. Jacob Leed (Kent, Ohio, 1966), pp. 79–106.

terpretive inferences can be drawn from the material?" (p. 104). The answer comes in two parts and illustrates the two basic maneuvers executed by the stylisticians. The first is circular: "The low frequency of initial determiners, taken together with the high frequency of initial connectives, makes [Swift] a writer who likes transitions and made much of connectives" (p. 104). As the reader will no doubt have noticed, the two halves of this sentence present the same information in slightly different terms, even though its rhetoric suggests that something has been explained. Here is an example of what makes some people impatient with stylistics and its baggage. The machinery of categorization and classification merely provides momentary pigeonholes for the constituents of a text, constituents which are then retrieved and reassembled into exactly the form they previously had. There is in short no gain in understanding; the procedure has been executed, but it hasn't gotten you anywhere. Stylisticians, however, are *determined* to get somewhere, and exactly where they are determined to get is indicated by Milic's next sentence. "[Swift's] use of series argues [that is, is a sign of or means] a fertile and well stocked mind." Here the procedure is not circular but arbitrary. The data are scrutinized and an interpretation is *asserted* for them; asserted rather than proven because there is nothing in the machinery Milic cranks up to authorize the leap (from the data to a specification of their value) he makes. What does authorize it is an unexamined and highly suspect assumption that one can read directly from the description of a text (however derived) to the shape or quality of its author's mind, in this case from the sheer quantity of verbal items to the largeness of the intelligence that produced them.

The counterargument to this assumption is not that it can't be done (Milic, after all, has done it), but that it can be done all too easily, and in any direction one likes. One might conclude, for example, that Swift's use of series argues the presence of the contiguity disorder described by Roman Jakobson in *The Fundamentals of Language;* [2] or that Swift's use of series argues an unwillingness to finish his sentences; or that Swift's use of series argues an anal-retentive personality; or that Swift's use of series argues a nominalist rather than a realist philosophy and is therefore evidence of a mind insufficiently stocked with abstract ideas. These conclusions are neither more nor less defensible than the conclusion Milic reaches, or reaches for (it is the enterprise and not any one of its results that should be challenged), and their availability points to a serious defect in the procedures of stylistics, the absence of any constraint on the way in which one moves from description to interpretation, with the result that any interpretation one puts forward is arbitrary.

Milic, for his part, is not unaware of the problem. In a concluding paragraph, he admits that relating devices of style to personality is "risky" and "the chance of error . . . great" because "no personality syntax paradigm is available . . . neither syntactic stylistics nor personality theory is yet capable of making the leap" (p. 105). Once again Milic provides a clear

[2] Roman Jakobson and Morris Halle, *The Fundamentals of Language* (The Hague, 1955), pp. 69–96.

example of one of the basic manuevers in the stylistics game:
he acknowledges the dependence of his procedures on an unwarranted assumption, but then salvages both the assumption
and the procedures by declaring that time and the collection
of more data will give substance to the one and authorize the
other. It is a remarkable *non sequitur* in which the suspect nature of his enterprise becomes a reason for continuing in it: a
personality syntax paradigm may be currently unavailable or
available in too many directions, but this only means that if we
persist in our efforts to establish it, it will surely emerge. The
more reasonable inference would be that the difficulty lies not
with the present state of the art but with the art itself; and
this is precisely what I shall finally argue, that the establish-
ment of a syntax-personality or of any other paradigm is an
impossible goal, which, because it is also an assumption, invalidates the procedures of the stylisticians before they begin,
dooming them to successes that are meaningless because they
are so easy.

Milic affords a particularly good perspective on what stylisticians do because his assumptions, along with their difficulties,
are displayed so nakedly. A sentence like "Swift's use of series
argues a fertile and well stocked mind" doesn't come along
very often. More typically, a stylistician will interpose a formidable apparatus between his descriptive and interpretive acts,
thus obscuring the absence of any connection between them.
For Richard Ohmann, that apparatus is transformational grammar and in "Generative Grammars and the Concept of Literary Style" he uses it to distinguish between the prose of Faulk-

ner and Hemingway.[3] Ohmann does this by demonstrating that Faulkner's style is no longer recognizable when "the effects of three generalized transformations"—the relative clause transformation, the conjunction transformation, and the comparative transformation—are reversed. "Denatured" of these transformations, a passage from "The Bear," Ohmann says, retains "virtually no traces of . . . Faulkner's style" (p. 142). When the same denaturing is performed on Hemingway, however, "the reduced passage still sounds very much like Hemingway. Nothing has been changed that seems crucial" (p. 144). From this, Ohmann declares, follow two conclusions: (1) Faulkner "leans heavily upon a very small amount of grammatical apparatus" (p. 143); and (2) the "stylistic difference . . . between the Faulkner and Hemingway passages can be largely explained on the basis of [the] . . . apparatus" (p. 145). To the first of these I would reply that it depends on what is meant by "leans heavily upon." Is this a statement about the apparatus or about the actual predilection of the author? (The confusion between the two is a hallmark of stylistic criticism.) To the second conclusion I would object strenuously, if by "explained" Ohmann means anything more than made formalizable. That is, I am perfectly willing to admit that transformational grammar provides a better means of fingerprinting an author than would a measurement like the percentage of nouns

[3] "Generative Grammars and the Concept of Literary Style," in *Contemporary Essays on Style,* ed. Glen A. Love and Michael Payne (Glenview, Ill., 1969), pp. 133–48. This essay originally appeared in *Word,* XX (December, 1964), 423–39.

or the mean length of sentences; for since the transformational model is able to deal not only with constituents but with their relationships, it can make distinctions at a structural, as opposed to a merely statistical, level. I am not willing, however, to give those distinctions an independent value, that is, to attach a fixed significance to the devices of the fingerprinting mechanism, any more than I would be willing to read from a man's actual fingerprint to his character or personality.

But this, as it turns out, is exactly what Ohmann wants to do. "The move from formal description of styles to . . . interpretation," he asserts, "should be the ultimate goal of stylistics," and in the case of Faulkner, "it seems reasonable to suppose that a writer whose style is so largely based on just these three semantically related transformations demonstrates in that style a certain conceptual orientation, a preferred way of organizing experience" (p. 143). But Faulkner's style can be said to be "based on" these three transformations only in the sense that the submission of a Faulkner text to the transformational apparatus yields a description in which they dominate. In order to make anything more out of this, that is, in order to turn the description into a statement about Faulkner's conceptual orientation, Ohmann would have to do what Noam Chomsky so pointedly refrains from doing, assign a semantic value to the devices of his descriptive mechanism, so that rather than being neutral between the processes of production and reception, they are made directly to reflect them. In the course of this and other essays, Ohmann does just that, finding, for example, that Lawrence's heavy use of deletion transformations is responsible for the "driving insistence one feels in reading" him,[4] and that Conrad's structures of chaining reflect his tendency to "link one thing with another associatively," [5] and that Dylan Thomas's breaking of selectional rules serves his "vision of things" of "the world as process, as interacting forces and repeating cycle"; [6] in short—and here I quote— "that these syntactic preferences *correlate* with habits of meaning." [7]

The distance between all of this and "Swift's use of series argues a fertile and well stocked mind" is a matter only of methodological sophistication, not of substance, for both critics operate with the same assumptions and nominate the same goal, the establishing of an inventory in which formal items will be linked in a fixed relationship to semantic and psychological values. Like Milic, Ohmann admits that at this point his interpretive conclusions are speculative and tentative; but again, like Milic, he believes that it is only a matter of time before he can proceed more securely on the basis of a firm correlation between syntax and "conceptual orientation," and the possibility of specifying such correlations, he declares, "is one of the main justifications for studying style." [8] If this is so, then the enterprise is in trouble, not because it will fail, but because it will, in every case, succeed. Ohmann will always be

[4] *Ibid.*, p. 148.
[5] "Literature as Sentences," in *Contemporary Essays on Style*, p. 154. This essay originally appeared in *College English*, XXVII (January, 1966), 261–67.
[6] *Ibid.*, p. 156.
[7] *Ibid.*, p. 154.
[8] "Generative Grammars and the Concept of Literary Style," p. 143.

able to assert (although not to prove) a plausible connection between the "conceptual orientation" he discerns in an author and the formal patterns his descriptive apparatus yields. But since there is no warrant for that connection in the grammar he appropriates, there is no constraint on the manner in which he makes it, and therefore his interpretations will be as arbitrary and unverifiable as those of the most impressionistic of critics.

The point will be clearer, I think, if we turn for a moment to the work of J. P. Thorne, another linguist of the generative persuasion. While Ohmann and Milic are interested in reading from syntax to personality, Thorne would like to move in the other direction, from syntax to either content or effect, but his procedures are similarly illegitimate. Thorne begins in the obligatory way, by deploring the presence in literary studies of "impressionistic terms."[9] Yet, he points out, these terms must be impressions of something, and what they are impressions of, he decides, "are types of grammatical structures." It follows from this that the task of stylistics is to construct a typology that would match up grammatical structures with the effects they invariably produce: "If terms like 'loose', or 'terse' or 'emphatic' have any significance . . . —and surely they do—it must be because they relate to certain identifiable structural properties" (pp. 188–89). What follows is a series of analyses in which "identifiable structural properties" are correlated with impressions and impressionistic terms. Thorne

[9] J. P. Thorne, "Generative Grammar and Stylistic Analysis," in *New Horizons in Linguistics*, ed. John Lyons (Baltimore, 1970), p. 188.

discovers, for example, that in Donne's "A Nocturnal Upon St. Lucie's Day" selectional rules are regularly broken. "The poem has sentences which have inanimate nouns where one would usually expect to find animate nouns, and animate nouns . . . where one would expect to find inanimate nouns." "It seems likely," he concludes, "that these linguistic facts underlie the sense of chaos and the breakdown of order which many literary critics have associated with the poem" (p. 193). This is at once arbitrary and purposeful. The "breakdown of order" exists only within his grammar's system of rules (and strange rules they are, since there is no penalty for breaking them); it is a formal, not a semantic fact (even though the rules are semantic), and there is no warrant at all for equating it with the "sense" the poem supposedly conveys. That sense, however, has obviously been preselected by Thorne and the critics he cites, and is, in effect, responsible for its own discovery. In other words, what Thorne has done is scrutinize his data until he discerns a "structural property" which can be made to fit his preconceptions. The exercise is successful, but it is also circular.[10]

It is not my intention flatly to deny any relationship between structure and sense, but to argue that if there is one, it is not to be explained by attributing an independent meaning to the linguistic facts, which will, in any case, mean differently in different circumstances. Indeed these same facts—animate

[10] For other examples of Thorne's work, see "Stylistics and Generative Grammars," *Journal of Linguistics*, I (1965), 49–59; "Poetry, Stylistics and Imaginary Grammars," *Journal of Linguistics*, V (1969), 147–50.

nouns where one expects inanimate and inanimate where one expects animate—characterize much of Wordsworth's poetry, where the sense communicated is one of harmony rather than chaos. Of course, counterexamples of this kind do not prove that a critic is wrong (or right) in a particular case, but that the search for a paradigm of formal significances is a futile one. Those who are determined to pursue it, however, will find in transformational grammar the perfect vehicle; for since its formalisms operate independently of semantic and psychological processes (are neutral between production and reception) they can be assigned any semantic or psychological value one may wish them to carry. Thus Ohmann can determine that in one of Conrad's sentences the deep structural subject "secret sharer" appears thirteen times and conclude that the reader who understands the sentence must "register" what is absent from its surface; [11] while Roderick Jacobs and Peter Rosenbaum can, with equal plausibility, conclude that the presence of relative clause reduction transformations in a story by John Updike results "in a very careful suppression of any mention of individual beings" as agents.[12] In one analysis the grammatical machinery is translated into an activity the reader must perform; in the other it prevents him from performing that same activity. This is a game that is just too easy to play.

It is possible, I suppose, to salvage the game, at least temporarily, by making it more sophisticated, by contextualizing it. One could simply write a rule that allows for the different

[11] "Literature as Sentences," pp. 152–53.
[12] Roderick A. Jacobs and Peter S. Rosenbaum, *Transformations, Style and Meaning* (Waltham, Mass., 1971), pp. 103–6.

valuings of the same pattern by taking into account the features which surround it in context. But this would only lead to the bringing forward of further counterexamples and the continual and regressive rewriting of the rule. Eventually a point would be reached where a separate rule was required for each and every occurrence; and at that point the assumption that formal features *possess* meaning would no longer be tenable, and the enterprise of the stylisticians—at least as they conceive it—will have been abandoned.[13]

One can be certain, however, that it will not be abandoned, partly because the lure of "solid science" and the promise of an automatic interpretive procedure is so great, and partly because apparent successes are so easy to come by. For a final and spectacular example I turn to Michael Halliday and an article entitled "Linguistic Function and Literary Style." [14] Hal-

[13] My argument here has affinities with Hubert Dreyfus's explanation (in *What Computers Can't Do* [New York, 1972]) of the impasse at which programmers of artificial intelligence find themselves. "The programmer must either claim that some features are intrinsically relevant and have a fixed meaning regardless of content . . . or the programmer will be faced with an infinite regress of contexts" (p. 133). Dreyfus's conclusion anticipates the proposal I will offer at the end of this essay for the reform of stylistics. "Human beings seem to embody a third possibility which would offer a way out of this dilemma. Instead of a hierarchy of contexts, the present situation is recognized as a continuation or modification of the present one. Thus we carry over from the immediate past a set of anticipations based on what was relevant and important a moment ago. This carry-over gives us certain predispositions as to what is worth noticing" (p. 134).

[14] "Linguistic Function and Literary Style," in *Literary Style: A Symposium*, ed. Seymour Chatman (New York, 1971), pp.

liday is the proprietor of what he calls a category-scale grammar, a grammar so complicated that a full explanation would take up more space than I have. Allow me, however, to introduce a few of the basic terms. The number of categories is four: unit, structure, class, and system. Two of these, unit and structure, are categories of chain; that is, they refer to the syntagmatic axis or axis of combination. The category of unit relates the linear constituents of discourse to one another as they combine; representative units are morpheme, word, group, clause, and sentence. The category of structure is concerned with the syntagmatic relationships within units: subject, complements, adjunct, and predicator are elements of structure. The other two categories are categories of choice, of the paradigmatic axis or the axis of selection. The category of class contains those items which can be substituted for one another

---

330–65. See also Halliday, "Categories of the theory of grammar," *Word*, XVII (1961), 241–92; "The Linguistic Study of Literary Texts," in *Proceedings of the Ninth International Congress of Linguists*, ed. H. Hunt (The Hague, 1964), pp. 302–7; "Descriptive Linguistics in Literary Studies," in *Linguistics and Literary Style*, ed. Donald C. Freeman (New York, 1970), pp. 57–72; "Notes on Transitivity and Theme in English," *Journal of Linguistics*, III (1967), 37–81, 199–244, and *Journal of Linguistics*, IV (1968, 179–215; "Language Structure and Language Function," in *New Horizons in Linguistics*, ed. John Lyons (Baltimore, 1970), pp. 140–65. For an exposition of Halliday's grammar and its application to literary analysis, see John Spencer and Michael J. Gregory, "An Approach to the Study of Style," in *Linguistics and Literary Style* (London, 1964), pp. 59–105. For a critique of the tradition in which Halliday works, see D. T. Langendoen, *The London School of Linguistics* (Cambridge, Mass., 1968).

at certain points in a unit; classes include nouns, verbs, and adjectives. The category of system refers to the systematic relationships between elements of structure, relationships of agreement and difference, such as singular and plural, active and passive. Together, these categories make it possible for the linguist to segment his text either horizontally or vertically; that is, they make possible an exhaustive taxonomy.

This, however, is only part of the story. In addition, Halliday introduces three scales of abstraction which link the categories to each other and to the language data. They are rank, exponence, and delicacy. The scale of rank refers to the operation of units within the structure of another unit: a clause, for example, may operate in the structure of another clause, or of a group, or even of a word, and these would be first, second, and third degree rank shifts, respectively. Exponence is the scale by which the abstractions of the system relate to the data: it allows you to trace your way back from any point in the descriptive act to the actual words of a text. And finally the scale of delicacy is the degree of depth at which the descriptive act is being performed. While in some instances one might be satisfied to specify at the level of a clause or a group, in a more delicate description one would want to describe the constituents and relationships within those units themselves.

If this were all, the apparatus would be formidable enough; but there is more. Halliday also adopts, with some modifications, Karl Bühler's tripartite division of language into three functions—the ideational function or the expression of content; the interpersonal function, the expression of the speaker's attitudes and evaluations, and of the relationships he sets up between himself and the listener; and the textual function, through which language makes links with itself and with the extralinguistic situation.[15] Obviously these functions exist at a different level of abstraction from each other and from the taxonomic machinery of categories and scales, and just as obviously they create a whole new set of possible relationships between the items specified in that taxonomy; for as Halliday himself remarks, in a statement that boggles the mind with its mathematical implications, "each sentence embodies all functions . . . and most constituents of sentences also embody more than one function." [16]

The result is that while the distinctions one can make with the grammar are minute and infinite, they are also meaningless, for they refer to nothing except the categories of the system that produced them, categories which are themselves unrelated to anything outside their circle except by an arbitrary act of assertion. It follows, then, that when this grammar is used to analyze a text, it can legitimately do nothing more than provide labels for its constituents, which is exactly what Halliday does to a sentence from *Through the Looking Glass:* "It's a poor sort of memory that only works backwards." Here is the analysis:

The word *poor* is a "modifier," and thus expresses a subclass of its head word *memory* (ideational); while at the same time it is an "epithet" expressing the Queen's attitude (interpersonal), and the choice of this word in this environment

[15] "Linguistic Function and Literary Style," p. 339.
[16] *Ibid.,* p. 334.

(as opposed to, say, useful) indicates more specifically that the attitude is one of disapproval. The words *it's . . . that* have here no reference at all outside the sentence, but they structure the message in a particular way (textual), which represents the Queen's opinion as if it were an "attribute" (ideational), and defines one class of *memory* as exclusively possessing this undesirable quality (ideational). The lexical repetition in *memory that only works backwards* relates the Queen's remark (textual) to *mine only works one way* in which *mine* refers anaphorically, by ellipsis, to *memory* in the preceding sentence (textual) and also to *I* in Alice's expression of her own judgment *I'm sure* (interpersonal). Thus ideational content and personal interaction are woven together with, and by means of, the textual structure to form a coherent whole. (p. 337)

What, you might ask, is this coherent whole? The answer is, "It's a poor sort of memory that only works backwards." But that, you object, is what we had at the beginning. Exactly. When a text is run through Halliday's machine, its parts are first disassembled, then labeled, and finally recombined into their original form. The procedure is a complicated one, and it requires a great many operations, but the critic who performs them has finally done nothing at all.

Halliday, however, is determined to do something, and what he is determined to do is confer a value on the formal distinctions his machine reads out. His text is William Golding's *The Inheritors*, a story of two prehistoric tribes one of which supplants the other. The two tribes—the "people" and the "new people," respectively—are distinguished not only by their activities but by their respective languages, and these, in turn, are distinguishable from the language of the reader. Language A, the language of the "people," is, according to Halliday, dominant for more than nine tenths of the novel. Here is a sample of it:

> The man turned sideways in the bushes and looked at Lok along his shoulder. A stick rose upright and there was a lump of bone in the middle. Lok peered at the stick and the lump of bone and the small eyes in the bone things over the face. Suddenly Lok understood that the man was holding the stick out to him but neither he nor Lok could reach across the river. He would have laughed were it not for the echo of screaming in his head. The stick began to grow shorter at both ends. Then it shot out to full length again. The dead tree by Lok's ear acquired a voice. "Clop." His ears twitched and he turned to the tree. By his face there had grown a twig. (p. 360)

From this and other samples Halliday proceeds to a description of the people's language, using the full apparatus of his category-scale grammar; but what begins as a description turns very quickly into something else:

> The clauses of passage A . . . are mainly clauses of action . . . location . . . or mental process . . . the remainder are attributive. . . . Almost all of the action clauses . . . describe simple movements . . . and of these the majority . . . are intransitive. . . . Even such normally transitive verbs as *grab* occur intransitively. . . . Moreover a high proportion . . . of the subjects are not people; they are either parts of the body . . . or inanimate objects . . . and of the human

subjects half again . . . are found in clauses which are not clauses of action. Even among the four transitive action clauses . . . one has an inanimate subject and one is reflexive. There is a stress set up, a kind of syntactic counterpoint, between verbs of movement in their most active and dynamic form . . . and the preference for non-human subjects and the almost total absence of transitive clauses. (pp. 349–50)

Here, of course, is where the sleight of hand begins. To label a verb "active" is simply to locate it in a system of formal differences and relationships within a grammar; to call it "dynamic" is to semanticize the label, and even, as we see when the description continues, to moralize it:

It is particularly the lack of transitive clauses of action with human subjects . . . that creates an atmosphere of ineffectual activity; the scene is one of constant movement, but movement which is as much inanimate as human and in which only the mover is affected. . . . The syntactic tension expresses this combination of activity and helplessness. No doubt this is a fair summary of the life of Neanderthal man. (pp. 349–50)

This paragraph is a progression of illegitimate inferences. Halliday first gives his descriptive terms a value, and then he makes an ideogram of the patterns they yield. Moreover, the content of that ideogram—the Neanderthal mentality—is quite literally a fiction (one wonders where he got his information), and it is therefore impossible that these or any other forms should express it.

What happens next is predictable. The novel receives a Dar-

winian reading in which the grammatically impoverished
"people" are deservedly supplanted by the "new people"
whose fuller transitivity patterns are closer to our own: "The
transitivity patterns . . . are the reflexion of the underlying
theme . . . the inherent limitations of understanding of Lok
and his people and their consequent inability to survive when
confronted with beings at a higher stage of development" (p.
350). The remainder of the essay is full of statements like this;
the verbal patterns "reflect" the subject matter, are "con-
gruent" with it, "express" it, "embody" it, "encode" it, and at
one point even "enshrine" it. The assumption is one we have
met before—"syntactic preferences correlate with habits of
meaning"—but here it is put into practice on a much
grander scale: "The 'people's' use of transitivity patterns argues
a Neanderthal mind."

In short, when Halliday does something with his apparatus,
it is just as arbitrary as what Milic and Ohmann and Thorne
do with theirs. But why, one might ask, is he arbitrary in this
direction? Given the evidence, at least as he marshals it, the
way seems equally open to an Edenic rather than a Darwinian
reading of the novel, a reading in which the language of the
"people" reflects (or embodies or enshrines) a lost harmony between man and an animate nature. The triumph of the "new
people" would then be a disaster, the beginning of the end, of
a decline into the taxonomic aridity of a mechanistic universe.
There are two answers to this question, and the first should
not surprise us. Halliday's interpretation precedes his gathering
and evaluating of the data, and it, rather than any ability of
the syntax to embody a conceptual orientation, is responsible

for the way in which the data are read. There is some evidence that the interpretation is not his own (he refers with approval to the "penetrating critical study" of Mark Kinkead-Weakes and Ian Gregor), but whatever its source—and this is the second answer to my question—its attraction is the opportunity it provides him to make his apparatus the hero of the novel. For in the reading Halliday offers, the deficiencies of the "people" are measured by the inability of their language to fill out the categories of his grammar. Thus when he remarks that "in Lok's understanding the complex taxonomic ordering of natural phenomena that is implied by the use of defining modifiers is lacking, or . . . rudimentary" (p. 352), we see him sliding from an application of his system to a judgment on the descriptions it yields; and conversely, when the "new people" win out, they do so in large part because they speak a language that requires for its analysis the full machinery of that system. Not only does Halliday go directly from formal categories to interpretation, but he goes to an interpretation which proclaims the superiority of his formal categories. The survival of the fittest tribe is coincidental with a step toward the emergence of the fittest grammar. Whether Golding knew it or not, it would seem that he was writing an allegory of the ultimate triumph of Neo-Firthian man.

Is there, then, no point to Halliday's exercise? Are the patterns he uncovers without meaning? Not at all. It is just that the explanation for that meaning is not the capacity of a syntax to express it, but the ability of a reader to confer it. Golding, as Halliday notes, prefaces *The Inheritors* with an excerpt

from H. G. Wells's discussion of Neanderthal Man. As a result, we enter the story expecting to encounter a people who
differ from us in important respects, and we are predisposed to
attach that difference to whatever in their behavior calls attention to itself. It is in this way that the language of the "people"
becomes significant, not because it is symbolic, but because it
functions in a structure of expectations, and it is in the context
of that structure that a reader is moved to assign it a value.
The point is one that Halliday almost makes, but he throws it
away, on two occasions; first when he remarks that the reader's entrance into the novel requires a "considerable effort of
interpretation" (p. 348), and later when he specifies the nature
of that effort: "the difficulties of understanding are at the level
of interpretation—or rather . . . of re-interpretation, as
when we insist on translating 'the stick began to grow shorter
at both ends' as 'the man drew the bow'" (p. 358). Here I
would quarrel only with the phrase "we insist"; for the decision to reinterpret is not made freely; it is inseparable from the
activity of reading (the *text* insists), and the effort expended in
the course of that activity becomes the measure and sign of the
distance between us and the characters in the novel. In other
words, the link between the language and any sense we have
of Neanderthal Man is fashioned in response to the demands of
the reading experience; it does not exist prior to that experience, and in the experience of another work it will not be
fashioned, even if the work were to display the same formal
features. In any number of contexts, the sentence "the stick
grew shorter at both ends" would present no difficulty for a
reader; it would require no effort of reinterpretation, and

therefore it would not take on the meaning which that effort *creates* in *The Inheritors*. Halliday's mistake is not to assert a value for his data but to locate that value in a paradigm and so bypass the context in which it is actually acquired.

This goes to the heart of my quarrel with the stylisticians: in their rush to establish an inventory of fixed significances, they bypass the activity in the course of which significances are, if only momentarily, fixed. I have said before that their procedures are arbitrary, and that they acknowledge no constraint on their interpretations of the data. The shape of the reader's experience is the constraint they decline to acknowledge. Were they to make that shape the focus of their analyses, it would lead them to the value conferred by its events. Instead they proceed in accordance with the rule laid down by Martin Joos: "Text signals its own structure," [17] treating the deposit of an activity as if it were the activity itself, as if meanings arose independently of human transactions. As a result, they are left with patterns and statistics that have been cut off from their animating source, banks of data that are unattached to anything but their own formal categories, and are therefore, quite literally, meaningless.

In this connection it is useful to turn to a distinction made by John Searle, between institutional facts—facts rooted in a recognition of human purposes, needs, and goals—and brute facts—facts that are merely quantifiable. "Imagine," says Searle,

[17] Martin Joos, "Linguistic Prospects in the United States," in *Trends in European and American Linguistics* (Utrecht, 1961), p. 18.

a group of highly trained observers describing a . . . football game in statements only of brute facts. What could they say by way of description? Well, within certain areas a good deal could be said, and using statistical techniques certain "laws" could even be formulated . . . we can imagine that after a time our observers would discover the law of periodic clustering: at regular intervals organisms in like colored shirts cluster together in roughly circular fashion. . . . Furthermore, at equally regular intervals, circular clustering is followed by linear clustering . . . and linear clustering is followed by the phenomenon of linear interpenetration. . . . But no matter how much data of this sort we imagine our observers to collect and no matter how many inductive generalizations we imagine them to make from the data, they still have not described football. What is missing from their description? What is missing are . . . concepts such as touchdown, offside, game, points, first down, time out, etc. . . . The missing statements are precisely what describes the phenomenon on the field *as a game of football*. The other descriptions, the description of the brute facts can [only] be explained in terms of the institutional facts.[18]

In my argument the institutional facts are the events that are constitutive of the specifically human activity of reading, while the brute facts are the observable formal patterns that can be discerned in the traces or residue of that activity. The stylisticians are thus in the position of trying to do what Searle says cannot be done: explain the brute facts without reference

[18] John Searle, *Speech Acts: An Essay in the Philosophy of Language* (Cambridge, 1969), p. 52.

to the institutional facts which give them value. They would specify the meaning of the moves in the game without taking into account the game itself. Paradoxically, however, this gap in their procedures does not hamper but free them; for while it is true, as Hubert Dreyfus has recently observed, that once the data have "been taken out of context and stripped of all significance, it is not so easy to give it back," [19] the corollary is that it is *very* easy to replace it with whatever significance you wish to bring forward. The result is interpretations that are simultaneously fixed and arbitrary, fixed because they are specified apart from contexts, and arbitrary because they are fixed, because it is in contexts that meaning occurs.

The stylisticians, of course, have an alternative theory of meaning, and it is both the goal of, and the authorization for, their procedures. In that theory, meaning is located in the inventory of relationships they seek to specify, an inventory that exists independently of the activities of producers and consumers, who are reduced either to selecting items from its storehouse of significances or to recognizing the items that have been selected. As a theory, it is distinguished by what it does away with, and what it does away with are human beings, at least insofar as they are responsible for creating rather than simply exchanging meanings. This is why the stylisticians almost to a man identify meaning with either logic or message or information, because these entities are "pure" and remain uninfluenced by the needs and purposes of those who traffic in them. I have been arguing all along that the goal of

[19] *What Computers Can't Do*, p. 200.

the stylisticians is impossible, but my larger objection is that it is unworthy, for it would deny to man the most remarkable of his abilities, the ability to give the world meaning rather than to extract a meaning that is already there.

This, however, is precisely what the stylisticians want to avoid, the protean and various significances which are attached, in context and by human beings, to any number of formal configurations. Behind their theory, which is reflected in their goal which authorizes their procedures, is a desire and a fear: the desire to be relieved of the burden of interpretation by handing it over to an algorithm, and the fear of being left alone with the self-renewing and unquantifiable power of human signifying. So strong is this fear that it rules their procedures even when they appear to be taking into account what I accuse them of ignoring. Michael Riffaterre is a case in point. In every way Mr. Riffaterre seems to be on the right side. He criticizes descriptive techniques that fail to distinguish between merely linguistic patterns and patterns a reader could be expected to actualize.[20] He rejects the attempts of other critics to endow "formal . . . categories . . . with esthetic and . . . ethical values." [21] He insists that the proper object of analysis is not the poem or message but the "whole act of communication." [22] He argues for the necessity of "following exactly the normal reading process," [23] and it is that process he

[20] "Criteria for Style Analysis," *Word*, XV (1959), 164.
[21] "Describing Poetic Structures," in *Structuralism*, ed. Jacques Ehrmann (New York, 1970), p. 197. This volume was originally published in 1966 as numbers 36 and 37 of *Yale French Studies*.
[22] *Ibid.*, p. 202.   [23] *Ibid.*, p. 203.

seeks to describe when he asks readers, or as he calls them, informants, to report on their experiences. Once the process is described, however, Riffaterre does something very curious: he empties it of its content.[24] That is, he discounts everything his readers tell him about what they were doing and retains only the points at which they were compelled to do it. The pattern that emerges, a pattern of contentless stresses and emphases, is then fleshed out by the interpretation he proceeds to educe.

In short, Riffaterre does exactly what the other stylisticians do, but he does it later: he cuts his data off from the source of value and is then free to confer any value he pleases. The explanation for this curious maneuver is to be found in his equation of meaning with message or information; for if the message is the meaning, a reader's activities can only be valued insofar as they contribute to its clear and firm reception; anything else is simply evidence of an unwanted subjectivity and must be discarded. While the reader is admitted into Riffaterre's procedures, there is no real place for him in the theory and he is sent away after he has performed the mechanical task of locating the field of analysis. In the end, Riffaterre is distinguished only by the nature of his diversionary machinery. Like the other stylisticians, he introduces a bulky apparatus which obscures the absence of any connection between his descriptive and interpretive acts; the difference is that his is precisely the apparatus that would supply the connection (it is not taxonomic but explanatory); but after introducing it, he eviscerates it.

[24] *Ibid.* See also "Criteria for Style Analysis," p. 164.

Richard Ohmann performs somewhat the same operation on an entire school of philosophy. In his most recent work, Ohmann has proposed literary applications to the Speech Act theory of J. L. Austin (*How to Do Things with Words*) and John Searle,[25] a theory that turns traditional philosophy around by denying the primacy and even the existence of pure or context-free statements, All utterances, argue Austin and Searle, are to be understood as instances of purposeful human actions which happen to require language for their performance. Some of these are promising, ordering, commanding, requesting, questioning, warning, stating, praising, greeting, etc. Even this abbreviated list should be enough to suggest the main contention of this school, which is captured in Searle's declaration that propositional acts do not occur alone.[26] What this means is that every utterance possesses an illocutionary force, an indication of the way it is to be taken (as a promise, threat, warning, etc.) and that no utterance is ever taken purely, without reference to an intention in a context. Thus, for example, the string of words "I will come" may, in different circumstances, be a promise, a threat, a warning, a predic-

[25] See, in addition to the essay by Ohmann appearing in this volume, "Speech Acts and the Definition of Literature," *Philosophy and Rhetoric*, IV (Winter, 1971), 1–19; "Speech, Action and Style," in *Literary Style: A Symposium*, ed. Seymour Chatman (New York, 1971), pp. 241–59; "Speech, Literature, and the Space Between," *New Literary History*, IV (Autumn, 1972), 47–64; "Instrumental Style: Notes on the Theory of Speech as Actions," in *Current Trends in Stylistics*, ed. Braj B. Kachru (Edmonton, 1972).

[26] *Speech Acts*, p. 25.

tion; but it will always be one of these, and it will never be just a meaning unattached to a situation. What an older theory would have called the pure semantic value of the utterance is in this theory merely an abstraction, which, although it can be separated out for the sake of analysis, has no separate and independent status. The various illocutionary lives led by "I will come" are not different handlings of the same meaning, they are different meanings. In Speech Act theory, there is only one semantic level, not two; detached from its illocutionary force, a sentence is just a series of noises. Illocutionary force *is* meaning. (This is obvious in the paradigm instances where the illocutionary force marker is explicit, that is, a part of the utterance, which certainly cannot be detached from itself.)

It is not my intention here to embrace this theory (although I am attracted to it) but to explain some of its terms, terms which Ohmann appropriates. He also distorts them, in two predictable directions. First of all, he takes the slice of the speech act that Searle insists cannot stand alone and gives it an independent status. He calls it the locutionary act—a designation he borrows from Austin—and endows it with a force of its own, the semantic force of logical and grammatical structures.[27] This locutionary act then becomes the basic level of a two-level system of significations. The second, and subsidiary, level is occupied by the inventory of illocutionary forces, which function more or less as a rhetoric of social conventions and intentions. Illocutionary force is thus dislodged from its primary position and reduced to a kind of *emphasis,*

[27] See "Speech, Action, and Style," pp. 249–50.

something that is added to a content which is detachable from it and survives its influence. Ohmann, in short, turns the major insight of the speech act philosophers on its head, precisely undoing what they have so carefully done. It is in a way a remarkable feat: he manages to take a theory rooted in the recognition of human meaning and make it assert the primacy of a meaning that is specifiable apart from human activities. He succeeds, in the face of great odds, in preserving the context-free propositional core that is necessary if there is to be a rationale for the procedures of stylistics,[28] and it is only a measure of his success that he is then able to define literature impossibly as "discourse without illocutionary force." [29]

[28] That is to say, stylistics requires that there be two separate systems—one of content or message, the other of everything else—which it is the stylistician's job to match up or correlate. Otherwise, they complain, there would be nothing for them to do. Ohmann is consistent in his dualism from his earliest writings—when his grammar was structural—to his "middle period"—when the deep-surface distinction of Transformational Grammar seemed to give new authorization to the form-content split—to the present day—when the illocutionary force–propositional content distinction serves the same need. See "Instrumental Style" (MS paging): "[In] the distinction between the unactivated meaning and the fully launched illocutionary act we have the kind of split required for style to exist" (4).

[29] "Speech Acts and the Definition of Literature," p. 13. The definition is impossible because discourse without illocutionary force would be discourse unrelated to the conventions of everyday speech and therefore discourse that was unintelligible (just a series of noises). To put it another way, the language of literature would be wholly discontinuous with the language we ordinarily speak, and in order to read it one would have to learn it from scratch.

I do not mean to suggest conscious intention on Ohmann's part, any more than I would argue that the stylisticians consciously perform illegitimate acts of interpretation which they then deliberately disguise. Indeed I take the performance of these acts as evidence of the extent to which they are unaware of their assumptions; for if they were true to their covert principles (as are, for example, the structuralists) [30] they would be content with the description of formal patterns and admit that the value-free operation of those patterns has always been their

---

(Of course there *are* special poetic vocabularies, for example, silver-age Latin, but these are always precisely parallel to, that is, parisitic on, everyday usage.) Ohmann seems aware of this difficulty in his definition, since he modifies it on the very next page, admitting that a literary work has illocutionary force, but declaring that it is "mimetic." These mimetic speech acts, however, turn out to be just like real ones, and it seems that this strange class has been instituted only to remedy the deficiency of the original definition.

[30] That is, like the stylisticians, the structuralists dislodge man from his privileged position as the originator of meanings, and locate meaning instead in the self-sufficient operation of a timeless formalism. The difference is that they do consciously what the stylisticians do inadvertently; they deliberately raise the implied antihumanism of other formalist methodologies to a principle. The parallel holds too in the matter of interpretation. Since the structuralists' goal is the system of signifiers—intelligibility rather than what is made intelligible—they either decline interpretation or perform it in such a way as to make its arbitrary contingent nature inescapable (for example, Roland Barthes in *S/Z*). Again the similarity with what the stylisticians do is less important than the self-consciousness with which it is done. One may disagree with the assumptions impelling the structuralists' enterprise, but one cannot accuse them of being unaware of those assumptions.

goal. But they are not so content and insist on leaping from those patterns to the human concerns their procedures exclude. The dehumanization of meaning may be the implication, as well as the result, of what they do; but it is not, I think, what they consciously *want* to do.

What we have then, is a confusion between methodology and intention, and it is a confusion that is difficult to discern in the midst of the pseudo-scientific paraphernalia the stylisticians bring to bear. I return to my opening paragraph and to a final paradox. While it is the program of stylistics to replace the subjectivity of literary studies with objective techniques of description and interpretation, its practitioners ignore what is *objectively* true—that meaning is not the property of a timeless formalism, but something acquired in the context of an activity—and therefore they are finally more subjective than the critics they would replace. For an open impressionism, they substitute the covert impressionism of anchorless statistics and self-referring categories. In the name of responsible procedures, they offer a methodized irresponsibility, and, as a result, they produce interpretations which are either circular—mechanical reshufflings of the data—or arbitrary—readings of the data that are unconstrained by anything in their machinery.

What makes this picture particularly disturbing is the unlikelihood of its changing; for among the favorite pronouncements of the stylisticians are two that protect them from confronting or even acknowledging the deficiencies of their operations. The first is: "Stylistic studies are essentially comparative." Properly understood, this article of faith is a covert admission of the charges I have been making. What the stylisticians compare are the statistics derived from applying their categories to a variety of texts; but since those categories are unattached to anything (are without meaning) the differences revealed by the statistics are purely formal, and the only thing one can legitimately do with them is compare them with each other. The weakness of the exercise is that it is without content, but this is also its strength, since it can be endlessly and satisfyingly repeated without hazarding assertions about meaning or value. It is when such assertions are hazarded that the stylisticians get into trouble, but at this point they are ready with a second article of faith: the apparent unreliability of our procedures is a condition of insufficient data. Thus while Lúbomir Doležel (to cite just one example) is forced to admit that "there are surprising contradictions in the various interpretations of style characteristics," he manages to escape the implications of his admission by hanging everything on a future hope: "All conclusions about the properties and nature of style characteristics, about the speaker type and text type, and about stylistic differences, are to be considered hypotheses that will be confirmed or refuted by the accumulation of vast empirical material." [31] But the accumulation of empirical material will make a difference only if the ability of human beings to confer meaning is finite and circumscribable within a statistical formula; if it is not, then the resulting data will do nothing more than trace out more fully the past performance of that

[31] "A Framework for the Statistical Analysis of Style," in *Statistics and Style*, ed. Lúbomir Doležel and Richard W. Bailey (New York, 1969), p. 22.

ability, rather than, as Doležel and others hope, make its future performances predictable. In other words, the statistics will never catch up with the phenomenon they seek to circumscribe. But one can avoid this realization simply by forever advancing the date when the availability of more data will make everything all right.[32] The failure of the basic assumption to prove itself is also the mechanism which assures its continuing life, and assures too that stylisticians will never come

---

[32] Indeed the stylisticians often make incredibly damaging admissions and then walk away from them as if their entire program were still intact. Two examples from the work of Manfred Bierwisch will have to suffice. In an article entitled "Semantics" written for *New Horizons in Linguistics* (ed. John Lyons), Bierwisch points out that a semantic theory will have to be able "to explain how one of the several meanings associated with a particular word or sentence is selected in accordance with a particular universe of discourse" (p. 183). He then admits that at the present time there seems no way precisely to formalize (i.e., make predictable) the process by which, for example, the various meanings of the word "group" are selected; but he can still conclude (with no warrant whatsoever) that "although little progress has yet been made in the systematic treatment of these problems, they do not seem to pose difficulties of principle" (p. 184). In another of his articles, the problem is not an unsupported conclusion but a conclusion he fails to make. The article is "Poetics and Lingustics" (in *Linguistics and Literary Style*, ed. Donald C. Freeman), and at the close of it Bierwisch points out that references in poems to other poems or to other universes of discourse (e.g., art history) "can never be expressed in an exhaustive linguistic semantics and . . . thus mark . . . the boundaries of a complete theory of poetic effect and style" (p. 112). The conclusion that he doesn't reach (although it seems inescapable) is that a theory with those limitations is of questionable value.

to terms with the theoretical difficulties of their enterprise.

If the enterprise is so troubled, if, in short, the things people say about stylistics aren't terrible enough, what is the remedy? What is the critic who is interested in verbal analysis to do? The answer to this question would be the substance of another essay, but it has been more than anticipated here, especially in my counteranalysis of *The Inheritors*. I do not, the reader will recall, deny that the the formal distinctions Halliday uncovers are meaningful; but where he assumes that they *possess* meaning (as a consequence of a built-in relationship between formal features and cognitive capacities), I would argue that they *acquire* it, and that they acquire it by virtue of their position in a structure of experience. The structure with which the stylisticians are concerned is a structure of observable formal patterns, and while such patterns do exist they are themselves part of a larger pattern the description of which is necessary for a determination of their value. Thus, for example, while it is certainly possible (as Halliday demonstrates) to specify the properties of the languages spoken by the tribes in *The Inheritors*, the significance of those properties is a function of their reception and negotiation by a reader who comes upon them already oriented in the direction of specific concerns and possessed of (or by) certain expectations. These concerns and expectations themselves arise in the course of a consecutive activity engaged in by a finite consciousness; and it is my contention that a characterization of that activity must precede, and by preceding control, the characterization of the formal features which become part of *its* structure. In short, I am calling not for the end of stylistics but for a new stylistics, what I have termed elsewhere an "affective" stylistics,[33] in which the focus of attention is shifted from the spatial context of a page and its observable regularities to the temporal context of a mind and its experiences.

Does this mean a return to the dreaded impressionism? Quite the reverse. The demand for precision will be even greater because the object of analysis is a process whose shape is continually changing. In order to describe that shape, it will be necessary to make use of all the information that formal characterizations of language can provide, although that information will be viewed from a different perspective. Rather than regarding it as directly translatable into what a word or a pattern *means*, it will be used more exactly to specify what a reader, as he comes upon that word or pattern, is *doing*, what assumptions he is making, what conclusions he is reaching, what expectations he is forming, what attitudes he is entertaining, in short, what acts he is being moved to perform. When Milic observes that in Swift's prose connectives are often redundant and even contradictory—concessives cheek by jowl with causals [34]—we can proceed from what he tells us to an account of what happens when a reader is alternately invited to anticipate a conclusion and asked to qualify it before

[33] See "Literature in the Reader: Affective Stylistics," *New Literary History*, II (Autumn, 1970), 123–62. See also *Self-Consuming Artifacts* (Berkeley and Los Angeles, 1972) and *Surprised by Sin: The Reader in Paradise Lost* (New York and London, 1967).

[34] Louis Milic, "Connectives in Swift's Prose Style," in *Linguistics and Literary Style*, ed. Donald C. Freeman, pp. 243–57.

it appears. When Ohmann declares that the syntactical deviance of Dylan Thomas's "A Winter's Tale," "breaks down categorical boundaries and converts juxtaposition into action," [35] the boundaries, if they exist, take the form of a reader's expectations and their breaking down is an action *he* performs, thereby fashioning for himself the "vision of things" which the critic would attribute to the language. And when Halliday demonstrates that in the language of the "people" in Golding's *The Inheritors*, agency is given not to human but to inanimate subjects ("the stick grew shorter at both ends"), we can extrapolate from his evidence to the interpretive effort demanded of the reader who must negotiate it. In each case, a statement about the shape of the data is reformulated as a statement about the (necessary) shape of response, and in the kind of analysis I propose, a succession of such shapes would itself be given shape by the needs and concerns and abilities of a consciousness moving and working in time.

Information about language can be turned into information about response even when the formalizations are unattached to specific texts. Searle's analyses of questions, commands, promises, etc., in terms of the roles they involve, the obligations they institute, and the needs they presuppose, allow us, indeed oblige us, to include these things in any account of what a reader of a question or command or promise understands. Thus when Joan Didion begins *Play It As It Lays* with the sentence "What makes Iago evil?," simply by taking the question in, the reader casts himself in the role of its answerer.

[35] "Literature as Sentences," p. 156.

Moreover, he is directed by the tense, aspect (frequentative), and semantic content of "makes" to play that role in the context of a continuing and public literary debate about causality and motivation (how different would it be were the question "Why is Iago evil?"); and he will respond, or so Miss Didion assumes, with one or more of the many explanations that have been offered for Iago's behavior.[36] That same reader, however,

[36] Let me take the opportunity this example offers to clarify what I mean by *the* reader or, as I have elsewhere termed him, the "informed" reader. There are at least four potential readers of this sentence: (1) the reader for whom the name Iago means nothing; (2) the reader who knows that Iago is a character in a play by Shakespeare; (3) the reader who has read the play; (4) the reader who is aware that the question has its own history, that everyone has had a whack at answering it, and that it has become a paradigm question for the philosophical-moral problem of motivation. Now each of these readers will assume the role of answerer because each of them (presumably) is a native speaker of English who knows what is involved in a felicitous question. (His knowledge is the content of Searle's formalizations.) But the precision with which that role is played will be a function of the reader's particular knowledge of Iago. That is, the reader who is a member of my fourth class will not only recognize that he is being asked to perform the activity of answering but will perform it in a very specific direction (and consequently the speaker's withdrawal from that direction will be felt by him all the more sharply). He will be my informed reader and I would want to say that his experience of the sentence will be not only different from, but better than, his less-informed fellows. Note that this is not a distinction between real and ideal readers; all the readers are real, as are all their experiences. Nor do I assume a uniformity of attitude and opinion among informed readers. Some readers may believe that Iago is motivated by jealousy, others that he is motiveless, still others that

will be made a little less comfortable in his role by the second sentence: "Some people ask." The effect of "some" is to divide the world into two groups, those who seek after reasons and causes and those who don't. The reader, of course, has already accepted the invitation extended by the prose to become a member of the first group, and, moreover, he has accepted it in assumed fellowship with the first-person voice. That fellowship is upset by the third sentence—"I never ask"—which is also a judgment on what the reader has been (involuntarily) doing. Reader and narrator are now on different sides of the question originally introduced by the latter, and the tension between them gives point and direction to the experience of what follows.

Little of what I have said about this paragrah would emerge from a formal characterization of its components, but in my description of its experience I have been able to make use of formal characterizations—of a Speech Act analysis of a question, of a logician's analysis of the properties of "some," of a philosopher's analysis of making something happen—by regarding their content as cues for the reader to engage in activities. What is significant about these activities is that they are

---

he is not evil but heroic. It is the ability of the reader to have an opinion (or even to know that having an opinion is what is called for), and not the opinion he has, which makes him informed in my sense; for then, no matter what opinion he has, he will have committed himself to considering the issues of motivation and agency. That commitment will be the *content* of his experience and it will not be the content of the experience of readers less informed than he.

interpretive; for this means that a procedure in which their characterization is the first order of business avoids the chief theoretical deficiency of stylistics as it is now practiced. I have repeatedly objected to the absence in the work of the stylisticians of any connection between their descriptive and interpretive acts. In the kind of stylistics I propose, *interpretive acts are what is being described;* they, rather than verbal patterns arranging themselves in space, are the content of the analysis. This is more than a procedural distinction; for at its heart are different notions of what it is to read which are finally different notions of what it is to be human. Implicit in what the stylisticians do is the assumption that to read is to put together discrete bits of meaning until they form what a traditional grammar would call a complete thought. In this view, the world, or the world of the text, is already ordered and filled with significances and what the reader is required to do is get them out (hence the question, "What did you get out of that?"). In short, the reader's job is to extract the meanings that formal patterns possess prior to, and independently of, his activities. In my view, these same activities are constitutive of a structure of concerns which is necessarily prior to any examination of meaningful patterns because it is itself the occasion of their coming into being. The stylisticians proceed as if there were observable facts that could first be described and then interpreted. What I am suggesting is that an interpreting entity, endowed with purposes and concerns, is, by virtue of its very operation, determining what counts as the facts to be observed; [37] and, moreover, that since this determining is not a

[37] Again my argument intersects with that of Dreyfus in *What Computers Can't Do:* "There must be some way of avoiding the

neutral marking out of a valueless area, but the extension of an already existing field of interests, it *is* an interpretation.

The difference in the two views is enormous, for it amounts to no less than the difference between regarding human beings as passive and disinterested comprehenders of a knowledge external to them (that is, of an *objective* knowledge) and regarding human beings as at every moment creating the experiential spaces into which a personal knowledge flows. It is also a difference in methodological responsibility and rigor, between a procedure which is from the very beginning organizing itself in terms of what is significant, and a procedure which has no obligatory point of origin or rest. That is, if one sets out to describe in the absence of that which marks out the field of description, there is no way of deciding either where to begin or where to stop, because there is no way of deciding what counts. In such a situation, one either goes on at random and forever (here we might cite the monumental aridity of Jakobson's analyses of Baudelaire and Shakespeare) or one stops when the accumulated data can be made to fit a preconceived interpretive thesis. It has seemed to many that these are the only alternatives, and that, as Roger Fowler has declared, the choice is between "mere description" or description performed

---

self-contradictory regress of contexts, or the incomprehensible notion of recognizing an ultimate context, as the only way of giving significance to independent, neutral facts. The only way out seems to be to deny the separation of fact and situation . . . to give up the independence of the facts and understand them as a product of the situation. This would amount to arguing that only in terms of situationally determined relevance are there any facts at all" (p. 136).

at the direction of a preformulated literary hunch.[38] I have been arguing for a third way, one which neither begs the question of meaning nor predecides it arbitrarily, but takes as its point of departure the interpretive activity (experience) by virtue of which meanings occur.

This, then, is the way to repair the ruins of stylistics, not by linking the descriptive and interpretive acts, but by making them one.[39] It is hardly necessary to say that this kind of analysis is not without problems, and the problems are for the most part a direct consequence of its assumptions about what it means to be human. It can have no rules in the sense of discovery procedures, since the contextualizing ability that char-

[38] Roger Fowler, *The Languages of Literature: Some Linguistic Contributions to Criticism* (London, 1971), pp. 38–39.

[39] The resulting "single-shot" procedure also spells the end of another distinction, the distinction between style and meaning. This distinction depends on the primacy of propositional content (that which it is the reader's job to extract), but in an analysis which has as its object the structure of the reader's experience, the achieving of propositional clarity is only one among many activities, and there is no warrant for making it the privileged center in relation to which all other activities are either appendages or excrescences. Rather than the traditional dichotomy between process and product (the how and the what), everything becomes process and nothing is granted the stability that would lead to its being designated "content." Thus there is only style, or, if you prefer, there is only meaning, and what the philosophers have traditionally called meaning becomes an abstraction from the total meaning experience. Describing that experience becomes the goal of analysis and the resulting shape is both the form and the content of the description. (This is a "monism" not open to the usual objection that it leaves you with nothing to do.)

acterizes being human is not circumscribed by its previous performances, performances which, while they constitute the
history of that ability, do not constitute its limits. Thus the
value a formal feature may acquire in the context of a reader's
concerns and expectations is local and temporary; and there is
no guarantee that the value–formal feature correlation that
obtains once will obtain again (although an awareness that it
has obtained once is not without interest or usefulness). All
you have when you begin is a sense of this finite but infinitely
flexible ability and a personal knowledge of what it means to
have it. You then attempt to project the course that ability
would take in its interaction with a specific text, using as the
basis of your projection what you know, and at the same time
adding to what you know by the very effort to make analytical use of it. There are other things that can help. Formal linguistic characterizations can help, if, as I have said, one views
their content as potential cues for the performing acts. Literary history can help, if one views its conventions in the
same way; a description of a genre, for example, can and
should be seen as a prediction of the shape of response. Other
minds can help, because they know what you know, but with
the same lack of distance between themselves and their knowledge which makes the effort so difficult. Analyses of percep-
tual strategy can help,[40] because they acquaint us with the past
performances of the ability we are trying to know. (Our

[40] I am thinking, for example, of the work of T. G. Bever. See
"Perceptions, Thought, and Language," in *Language Comprehen-
sion and the Acquisition of Knowledge*, ed. Roy O. Freedle and
John B. Carroll (New York, 1972), pp. 99–112.

trying is itself just such a performance.) Finally, however, you are left only with yourself and with the impossible enterprise of understanding understanding; impossible because it is endless, endless because to have reached an end is to have performed an operation that once again extends it beyond your reach. In short, this way lacks the satisfaction of a closed system of demonstration and is unable ever to prove anything, although, paradoxically, this makes rigor and precision more, not less, necessary; but these very deficiencies are the reverse side of its greatest virtue (in both the modern and Renaissance sense): the recognition that meaning is human.

TZVETAN TODOROV
Structuralism and Literature

*T*HERE IS an anomaly in my title which I should like
to point out at the start. Whatever the precise meaning
of this term may be, "structuralism" is a trend in the recent
development of several social sciences. Thus it makes sense to
speak of, let us say, anthropology and structuralism, or linguistics and structuralism. The parallelism disappears, however,
when we move to a combination of words like: literature and
structuralism. In the previous cases we could associate a distinct science with a specific approach; in the second instance, a
field of research, not a science, appears in the same order: literature, not literary science.

This anomaly is not one I have invented. In all the universi-
ties of the countries I am familiar with, the division of
departments reflects it: we have, side by side, linguistics, eco-
nomics, physics, psychology—and then suddenly heteroge-
neous names appear, such as "English literature," "French literature," "Russian literature," etc. Sciences on the one hand,
fields of inquiry on the other. Imagine the result if analogously
the college of natural sciences were divided into "department
of earth," "air department," "sea department," and imagine inside the "earth department" specialists arguing about the superiority of the physical, the chemical, or the geometrical

"method." But that is precisely what happens in, let us say, an English department where competition arises between those who prefer the psychoanalytical, the sociological, or the linguistic approach (that's what happens in France, at least).

The reason for this is clear: the study of literature has never been considered as a science in and of itself; of course, I am merely repeating a trivial fact. But its very triviality is a good starting point for me since the structural analysis of literature is nothing other than an attempt to transform literary studies into a scientific discipline. By this term, "scientific," I do not mean, of course, the use of a laboratory with white mice or of computers; I rather refer to its larger sense: a coherent body of concepts and methods aiming at the knowledge of underlying laws. In this respect the meaning of the word "structuralism" is different in our context from the meaning it has in anthropology or linguistics. The latter two are already existing sciences, and the structural method is just one among others. Thus in linguistics we have been witness to a conflict between structural (taxonomic) linguistics, and transformational linguistics. I will not, however, give to the term "structural" such a narrow definition: from my point of view, taxonomy and transformations may both be structural.

This ambition—the move from literature to its science, poetics—implies at least two important choices. In each one of them we have to deal with a different kind of resistance.

Firstly, since literature *itself* has to become the subject of an autonomous study, we may characterize our approach as internal, as opposed to external. By "external" I mean any approach which, although belonging to a specific science, reduces literature to the status of mere material which illustrates a subject other than itself. For instance, in a psychological approach to literature the real subject of the study is the psychic structure of the author—be it an Oedipus complex or a devastating ego. In a similar way a Marxist approach will usually deal *in fact* with the social structures contemporary with the events represented in the book or the life of the author. In each case literature is reduced to a mere means to the knowledge of something else (psychology, society); it, itself, is not really studied. Here we agree with other literary scholars and by this argument we meet the opposition of other social scientists who ignore the specific nature of literature.

The second important choice is an emphasis on theory as opposed to one on the mere description of individual literary works. Here we agree with the other social scientists but will be attacked by the traditional literary scholar. The most common stricture laid upon structural studies of literature is that they ignore the specific nature of the individual work of art, that they reduce its originality, its most precious quality, to abstract universal schemes. There is, as a matter of fact, a similar saying in medicine: There are no sicknesses, there are only sick men. Fortunately enough (and notwithstanding the truth of this statement at a certain level) medicine has not *followed* this precept, and physicians do not start the examination of the human body each time anew, as if they knew nothing about it: otherwise many more people would have died early. Or look at psychology: it is certain that in a way the psychology of one man is different from that of another; nevertheless a science of psychology exists which has organized a body of abstract concepts with only an approximate relevance to each individual. But in literary studies the risk of killing people by defending absurd views does not exist; so for a long time to come we shall certainly hear of the refusal to accept theory as essential to the study of literature. But in fact no literary scholar can avoid adhering to some theory of literature. The very use of descriptive terms, whatever they may be, implies one, in spite of protestations to the contrary. One can only choose between being conscious of his theory or not; and there are many more chances of making the theory better if you are aware of it.

Of course, understood in a similar manner, the structural analysis of literature is not a completely new phenomenon. It has a very long tradition, under the name of poetics, which has furnished many of the tools literary scholars use today: the labels which we attach to genres, to the elements of the work, to literary devices of all kinds. It is obvious that in a new poetics one must keep in mind the results of the work of innumerable scholars of the past. Nevertheless it remains true that it is mainly under the influence of, on the one hand, the Russian Formalists (whose recent discovery in the Western world we owe to Victor Erlich) and, on the other, structural analysis in linguistics and anthropology that the creation of poetics as a scientific discipline becomes possible today.

A very common error which one encounters in reading those who criticize literary structural analysis (that is, for me, poetics) is the confusion between the principles of this approach and its more or less successful practical application. During the last decade some inspiration was found, in this field, in the pioneering work of Vladimir Propp on folktales. Consequently many critics tell us: your schemes may apply to such simple literary genres as the folktale; but they are powerless before any literary masterpiece, be it Shakespeare or Dostoevsky, where the mere concatenation of events has little importance as compared to the subtleties of the narrative or dramatic discourse itself. But this is a misunderstanding; in fact the Russian Formalists started their analysis of fiction with a distinction between story and plot, that is, the events themselves and their mode of existence in the literary work, suggesting that only the latter properly belonged to the field of poetics; the inclusion of the "story" in the same realm is a more recent acquisition of structural analysis (exemplified by Propp) but it is in no sense a more legitimate one. As a matter of fact, one of the most brilliant analyses produced by the Formalist school was devoted precisely to Dostoevsky (here I refer to Bakhtin's magnificent study); and, incidentally, the series "Poetique" has published a structural analysis of a writer as far removed from the folktale as Proust, written by Gérard Genette.[1]

I recently read another critique of structural analysis in an article from which I quote a few sentences: "It appears that by this narrative device alone it is possible for the novel to declare itself to be of indeterminate structure and thus out of the bounds of structural analysis. . . . The profusion of plots, and the fundamental indeterminacy of the basic situation, are also indications that the 'structuralist' methods of analysis will fail

[1] Gérard Genette, *Figures III* (Paris, 1972).

to say anything very relevant or interesting." The idea is that a certain particular novel has an indeterminate structure; that structural analysis can only deal with determinate structures or, rather, that it determines all structures and thus betrays this particular one. But the exact reverse is true of structural analysis and in other reviews, more correctly, it is precisely the opposite feature that is criticized. A study in poetics is not in itself an interpretation of a particular work of art. It is rather concerned with identifying the characteristic features present in a work of art—those which are purely verbal, those that are compositional, thematic, rhythmic, narrative, etc.—and with showing their resemblances to and differences from other similar structures, in other works of art. Their structure may of course be indeterminate. I tried to show, several years ago,[2] that the whole genre of the *fantastic* was based on a certain indeterminacy, or rather a hesitation on the part of the implied reader; this is precisely its structure. But a structural analysis can never give us *the* meaning of a story, which is precisely the task of every different interpretation, according to the framework chosen by the critic. One may even reproach structural analysis for leaving all analyzed works in a state of indeterminacy: poetics can only invalidate wrong interpretations, it cannot produce the "right" one.

Although the proper subject of poetics is not the individual work but stylistic and narrative devices, themes, and genres in general, in practice our work cannot be imagined without a

[2] In my book *Introduction à la littérature fantastique* (Paris, 1970). In English cf. "The Fantastic in Fiction," *20th Century Studies*, III (1970), 76–92.

minute knowledge of existing novels and poems. However, the poetician, as I should like to call him, must always be aware that his final goal is the knowledge of literature, and not of this or that particular work. This latter activity, of *interpretation*, has its own techniques, its own methods, and the two are in a relation of mutual dependence.

Having suggested this very general framework I would like to turn briefly to a specific problem in poetics, which perhaps will bring us closer to the general topic of linguistics and literary study. But before we can discuss the relationship between language and literature we have to be sure how we mean these terms, particularly the term "literature." After all, the mere existence of a word is not a sufficient proof that it is required in a scientific theory. Of course we all know intuitively what literature is—namely, all the books discussed in classes on literature; however, once more, this is only the extension of a notion whose intention has still to be discovered. More specifically, the interesting question is to know whether literature can be characterized by internal properties and is therefore what we may call a structural entity, or whether it can be identified only by its functions, in a larger framework, and is thus what we may call a functional entity.

A definition of literature can only be valid if we are able to distinguish between what is literature and what is not, that is, if we can separate it from the other products of language. And all the existing definitions start with an opposition between literature and nonliterature. If we do not know what the fate of "literature" is, we can perhaps make up our minds concerning its opposite: this is not a scientific concept but a mere catchword. Can we by some simple expression such as "everyday use of language" or "descriptive (or assertive) writing" cover such contrasting verbal products as jokes and practical conversation, the ritual language of administration and law, scientific writings, and philosophical or religious books?

Things change radically if we introduce, instead of the catchword "nonliterature," the idea of a variety of discourses. A single utterance, one may say, is determined by a number of rules which form several distinct sets. At one pole there are the rules of language which produce all possible sentences. At the other there are the particular circumstances of each individual speech act, which determine in a definite way our verbal production. However, these two sets of rules are not separated by a desert: between them we find what I will call the rules of discourse. Whatever our language and whatever the particular circumstances, we do not write a scientific article in the same way in which we write a letter (and there are different kinds of letters, too); we all know the difference between jokes and mere gossip. We are never "just talking" since we always and necessarily obey the rules of a given type of discourse.

Let us turn back to literature now. We all have felt uncomfortable about definitions of literature such as "fictitious imitation" or "the words which must be, not mean." I wonder if an explanation for our uneasiness might not be that they apply to *kinds* of literature instead of defining it as a whole. For the words of a novel must certainly mean, and those of a poem need not create any fiction. One could go further and suggest that sometimes the similarities between some kinds of literature and some kinds of "nonliterature" are greater than those between the kinds within each rubric. For instance, there are more common points between a lyric poem and a prayer than between the former and *War and Peace*. Or between an imaginary voyage traditionally classified as literature and the description of a real voyage, supposed to be nonliterary: they resemble each other more than each resembles a lyric poem. And one cannot understand Joyce unless he studies also the techniques of the kind of word-play used in ordinary jokes.

What I am trying to suggest is this: instead of the uneasy dichotomy between literature and nonliterature we must introduce a typology of discourses. The generic level is, I believe, much less relevant than the specific. Accordingly, there is no reason other than tradition why we should study only literary discourse and not all the others too. There is a fruitful field of collaboration open to poeticians, rhetoricians, ethnographers of speech, philosophers of language, etc.

Thus the initial topic to which the expression "language and literature" might refer is transformed for me into the topic "language and discourse." Now what can we say about the relationship between these two terms? One may wonder if this very question does not force linguistics and linguistic models upon us. I am very conscious of this danger and believe that the description of a discourse must be conducted, to a certain degree, independently of the study of linguistic forms. Nevertheless, we cannot avoid questioning the nature of the link between language and discourse.

I will only sketch out a hypothesis on this subject without offering any proofs (these will eventually appear in a future volume). According to this hypothesis, language is not the

mere means of discourse but also its matrix. The relation between the two is not only functional but also genetic. Discour-
sive forms are transformations of linguistic forms. I shall illus-
trate this thesis by mentioning some studies which bear upon
this subject. As we shall see immediately, some important
choices still remain open, and one has not entirely determined
his position by adhering to the general thesis itself.

The Ukranian scholar A. A. Potebnya in his lectures during
the late 1800s at the University of Kharkov (published under
the title of *Iz lekeij po teorii slovesnosti. Basnja. Poslovica. Po-
govorka* [Kharkov, 1894]) was one of the first to inquire about
what one may call the *endogenesis* of literary works (as opposed to their *exogenesis* where the point of reference is
sought outside of the work itself: in the author's psychology,
or in the philosophical trends of the time). Potebnya observes
the close proximity of the genres which he studies (fables and
proverbs) and formulates the idea of a move from one form to
another by means of transformation: he speaks of the "unfolding" (*razvertyvanie*) of the proverb into a fable, and, conversely, of the "folding up" (*svertyvanie*) of the fable into a
common saying or a proverb (pp. 91-96). One can thus imagine that what was here the moral of a fable becomes there an
independent proverb. Notice that if the proverb may explain
the moral of the fable and, accordingly, its general intention, it
gives us no instructions concerning what precedes the moral: a
thousand roads can bring us to the same point of arrival. One
form literally participates in the other; but even if it determines the general movement of the latter, one cannot say that
the two resemble each other. The illustration of the moral

which is the heart of the fable is merely absent from the proverb. One is the concrete germ of the other, not its image.

The Russian Formalists have been influenced to a certain extent by Potebnya's research and one finds the same idea developed by Shklovsky. "The [narrative] motive is close to the trope and to puns," writes Shklovsky. "The plots of erotic stories are often 'unfolded' metaphors, for instance Boccaccio comparing the sexual organs of man and woman to mortar and pestle. This simile is motivated by a whole story and thus a motive is born. The same phenomenon may be observed in the novella about the devil and hell; only in this case the process of unfolding is still more obvious since at the end we are told frankly that there exists such a popular expression. A number of novellas are nothing else but the unfolding of a pun. Take for instance the stories of the origin of names." [3] Thus Shklovsky widens Potebnya's assertion without changing its framework. Not only can proverbs appear as the condensation of fables but also sayings ("send the devil to hell"), tropes ("mortar and pestle"), puns (Shklovsky's example is the name of the river *Okhta*) can play the same role in relation to a narrative. The general relationship remains the same, however: in the two cases the trope is identical but in the narrative it must be *motivated*, that is, introduced and justified by a story whose only fixed point is the end. The relationship is one of participation, not of similarity. We are not far from the old theory of Max Müller on myth origin according to which myths are *a posteriori* justifications of some particular linguistic forms (of "verbal accidents").

[3] *Théorie de la littérature* (Paris, 1965), p. 172.

The same point of view is explored more systematically by
the Soviet scholar G. L. Permyakov in a recent book whose
title is, interestingly enough, *From Saying to Tale* (*Ot pogo-
vorki do skazki* [Moscow, 1970]), with the subtitle "Notes on
the general theory of stereotypes" (clichés). This is a complete
classification of all verbal stereotypes, starting with idiomatic
expressions, ending with the bigger folklore genres: fairy tales,
didactic tales, fables; his classification covers all the aspects of
these forms: verbal, compositional, and thematic. Permyakov
summarizes his results in the following way: "Inevitably we
arrive at the conclusion that all the complex stereotypes from
idiomatic expressions to didactic tales set up a sequential series
of linguistic forms" (p. 75). "The differences between the units
within the sentence and beyond the sentence are quantitative"
(p. 56). In other terms, the larger forms grow up out of the
smaller. A possible explanation of this fact will be, according
to the author, that all these units function as signs of the same
real or imaginary situations, signs which give form to our perception of the world (p. 63). Permyakov's thesis is backed up
by numerous examples borrowed from the folklore genres of
different nations.

From this point of view a relationship is established between
a particular proverb and a concrete fable, between one metaphor and one tale. There also may be a second attitude in
which one confronts in an abstract and general manner linguistic and literary forms, without worrying about the existential reality of the relationship. May we still speak of endogenesis? I believe so, although the meaning of the term changes:

this is indeed an abstractly constructed genesis but it may help us better to understand the nature of each form.

This second version of the general hypothesis may be first illustrated by a statement of Diderot concerning the characteristics of drama: "The contrast of characters is to the construction of a play what antithesis is to speech." Shklovsky has formulated similar remarks. But it was the Dutch scholar André Jolles who first explicitly stated this theory in his book *Einfache Formen* (1930; I translate from the French translation, 1972). His analysis, applied to nine different genres, consists in "establishing in detail the movement which connects language and literature": starting with "the units and articulations of language such as they are elaborated by grammar, syntax and semantics"; passing through these intermediary "forms" which are the main subject of his book, such as legend, myth, riddle, proverb; and arriving at the proper literary forms as we actually find them in the "greatest works of art." According to Jolles, "to give an example, one could start with the syntactic figures of language and have as a final result the work composed by the artist" (p. 17).

I gave some other examples of this approach to the problem in an earlier study on language and literature; [4] I will not repeat them now. I would like to add just one more illustration: the relation between the system of grammatical cases and what

---

[4] "Language and Literature," in R. Macksey and E. Donato, eds., *The Structuralist Controversy* (Baltimore and London, 1970), pp. 125–33.

is presently called in France "modèle actantiel." A long the-
atrical tradition beginning with the *commedia dell' arte* demonstrates an idea, first stated by Gezzi, later elaborated by the
French aesthetician Etienne Souriau: namely, that the same
roles (or *emplois*) can be found in innumerable plays. Working
independently Propp has met the same problem in his study of
the Russian fairy tale: once again the roles and the "sphere of
action" are constant, though their identity may be hidden behind the apparent variety of concrete characters. Now Algir-
das Greimas, a contemporary French scholar, has noticed not
only the proximity of these two formulations but also the fact
that the set of relationships between the characters reproduces
the same categories as a system of grammatical cases. "Peter
gives an apple to Mary": these are not only instances of nomi-
native, accusative, and dative cases but also three possible roles
in a narrative: subject, object, and beneficiary (unless the beneficiary is a victim; for example, if Peter is the name of a snake,
and Mary, a proxy for Eve).

From this second point of view language and literature, or
language and discourse, are related again but in a different
way: we deal no longer with concrete occurrences but with abstract forms. The final result is not a particular text but a
genre, or a device, or some other category of literary discourse. Hence the relationship itself changes: instead of the direct participation, of the total inclusion of A into B where A
determines only the final point of B, we now have a relationship where there is no real filiation but rather a global iso-
morphism. Imagine a small slide projected onto a huge screen:

the appearances are quite different, but the relationships of the parts to each other remain the same. Analogously, the linguistic form appears to be an image of a whole literary genre.

These two attitudes, however different they may be, are not irreconcilable. The proof is given by certain studies which realize the conjunction of the two. The direct, concrete participation (as in the case of the proverb and the fable) may be reduplicated by a global repetition of the same figure. Roman Jakobson has often given examples of a metaphor or a simile which becomes both the pretext and the protoform of a narrative founded on a parallelism. In the same way structural resemblance (as in the case of grammatical cases and roles in a narrative or a drama) can be more than an abstract construction of an outside observer: it may coincide with a real filiation. Metonymy, or more precisely contiguous association, may be more than an image, more than a model of the narrative movement in general. As Gérard Genette has proved, in the case of Proust at least, the narrative starts literally at the moment when an initial analogy is replaced by a contiguous horizontal linkage. The same double relationship may be observed between the global structure of a literary genre, namely, the literature of fantasy, which entails an ambiguity between a natural and a supernatural interpretation of the same uncanny events, and verbal tropes which appear systematically in the stories of fantasy and which seem to contain the same ambiguity between their literal and transferred meaning. Thus the tropes realize both a direct relationship of participation (they are one of the means by which the fantastic takes place) and an indirect relationship of similarity: the trope, in a way, is a prefiguration of the structure of the whole genre. Once more factual and formal kinships are interrelated.

I am perfectly conscious of the fact that the mere enumeration of these examples does not satisfactorily replace the proofs by which I should back up my initial statement. Not only am I selecting isolated remarks instead of formulating an integrated system of arguments, but the initial terms whose very relationship I am trying to describe, the terms "language" and "discourse," are far from being clear and rigorous. Where does one end and the other begin? In order to render their subject homogeneous, linguists of the past have often excluded from the notion of language what we consider today to be some of its basic features. For Ferdinand de Saussure everything beyond the morpheme (that is, not only the utterance but even sentences and phrases) belongs to discourse (*parole*) and not to language (*langue*). No longer do contemporary linguists ignore the existence of syntax; but not long ago, in semantics, no place could be found for the metaphorical (or, more generally, tropical) creation of new meanings: we were told that "normally" words have one single meaning: ambiguity and metaphor were not to be found in any "serious" use of language but only in jokes or, precisely, in poetry. But is there language without metaphor?

Where does language end? and where does the discourse begin? At the present time we are still very unsure. But I believe that in our field the very raising of certain questions is in itself an important step. Good questions are perhaps more necessary right now than acceptable answers.

The English Institute, 1972
※

Northrop Frye, *Massey College, University of Toronto*
James M. Osborn, *Yale University*
William K. Wimsatt, *Yale University*

ARCHIVIST

David V. Erdman, *State University of New York, Stony Brook*, and *New York Public Library*

CHAIRMAN OF 1972 NOMINATING COMMITTEE

Helen Vendler

The Program

SATURDAY, SEPTEMBER 2, THROUGH TUESDAY, SEPTEMBER 5, 1972

I. POETS ON POETS
Directed by Daniel Hoffman, *University of Pennsylvania*

Sat.	1:45 P.M.	Wordsworth: The Absolute Self Mark Strand, author of *Darker; Brooklyn College, City University of New York*
Sun.	9:30 A.M.	Notes on Whitman Galway Kinnell, author of *The Book of Nightmares* and *Body Rags*
Sun.	11:00 A.M.	Emily Dickinson: Secrets of the Line Richard Howard, author of *Untitled Subjects* and *Findings*

II. NEW APPROACHES TO EIGHTEENTH-CENTURY LITERATURE
Directed by Phillip Harth, *University of Wisconsin*

Sat.	3:15 P.M.	The Future of Eighteenth-Century Literary Studies

Donald Greene, *University of Southern California*

Sun.   1:45 P.M.   The Use of the Concept of Genre in Eighteenth-Century Studies
Ralph W. Rader, *University of California, Berkeley*

Sun.   3:15 P.M.   Irony
Irvin Ehrenpreis, *University of Virginia*

III. RECENT LINGUISTICS AND LITERARY STUDY
Directed by Seymour Chatman, *University of California, Berkeley*

Mon.   9:30 A.M.   The Use of the Codes
Frank Kermode, *University College, University of London*

Mon.   11:00 A.M. Structuralism and Literature
Tzvetan Todorov, *Centre National de la Recherche Scientifique*

Tues.   9:30 A.M.   What Is Stylistics and Why Are They Saying Such Terrible Things About It?
Stanley Fish, *University of California, Berkeley*

Tues.   11:00 A.M. Literature as Act
Richard Ohmann, *Wesleyan University*

IV. REVALUATIONS OF T. S. ELIOT
Directed by A. Walton Litz, *Princeton University*

Mon.   1:45 P.M.   The Urban Apocalypse: *The Waste Land* Fifty Years After
Hugh Kenner, *University of California, Santa Barbara*

Mon.   3:15 P.M.   Eliot and "Modernity"
Robert M. Adams, *University of California, Los Angeles*

Tues.   1:45 P.M.   "Fear in the Way": Some Emotions in Eliot's Drama

Michael Goldman, *Queens College, City University of New York*

Tues.   3:15 P.M.   Anglican Eliot: The Later Poems

Donald Davie, *Stanford University*

Registrants, 1972

Maurianne Adams, Smith College; Robert M. Adams, University of California, Los Angeles; Ruth M. Adams, Dartmouth College; Burt Alimansky, University of California, Berkeley; Denison M. Allan, University of Hartford; Gellert S. Alleman, Rutgers University at Newark; Marcia Allentuck, City College, CUNY; Judith Anderson, Lowell State College; Judith H. Anderson, New Haven, Connecticut; Paul L. Andis, Transylvania University; J. A. Appleyard, Boston College; Jonathan Arac, Harvard University; Roy E. Aycock, Old Dominion University

George W. Bahlke, Kirkland College; Herschel Baker, Harvard University; C. L. Barber, University of California, Santa Cruz; James E. Barcus, Houghton College; Jonas A. Barish, University of California, Berkeley; Caroline K. Barnard, Morristown, New Jersey; Sister Marie Barry, s.n.d., Emmanuel College; J. Robert Barth, s.j., Harvard University; Bertrice Bartlett, Stephens College; Lynn C. Bartlett, Vassar College; Phyllis Bartlett, Queens College, CUNY; Maurice Beebe, Journal of Modern Literature; Charles F. M. Bellows, Pennsylvania State College; Josephine W. Bennett, Hunter College, CUNY; D. L. Bergdahl, Ohio Univer-

176   REGISTRANTS

sity; David E. Berndt, Boston University; Warner Berthoff, Harvard University; Paul Bertram, Rutgers University; Walter Bezanson, Rutgers University; Murray Biggs, Massachusetts Institute of Technology; Susan Blake, University of Connecticut; Bradley B. Blasdel, Los Angeles, California; Sophia B. Blaydes, West Virginia University; Kenneth A. Bleeth, Boston University; Sister M. Blish, Manhattanville College; Haskell M. Block, Brooklyn College, CUNY; Morton W. Bloomfield, Harvard University; Max Bluestone, University of Massachusetts at Boston; Charles R. Blyth, Cambridge, Massachusetts; Philip Bordinat, West Virginia University; George Bornstein, University of Michigan; Ruth Bowers, University of Connecticut; John D. Boyd, s.j., Fordham University; Robert Boyle, s.j., Marquette University; Barbara Breasted, Cambridge, Massachusetts; Martha M. Briney, Hood College; Leslie Brisman, Yale University; Cleanth Brooks, Yale University; Reuben A. Brower, Harvard University; Judith Brown, New York, New York; Marshall Brown, Boston University; Robert M. Browne, Université de Montréal; Jean R. Buchert, University of North Carolina at Greensboro; Jerome H. Buckley, Harvard University; Daniel Burke, f.s.c., La Salle College; Mary Fair Burks, University of Maryland, Eastern Shore; Sister M. Vincentia Burns, Albertus Magnus College; Douglas Bush, Harvard University; Andrew Busza, University of British Columbia; Francelia Butler, University of Connecticut

Daniel J. Cahill, University of Northern Iowa; Margot Callahan, University of Connecticut; John Cameron, Amherst College; Ruth A. Cameron, Eastern Nazarene College; James V. D. Card, Old Dominion University; Thomas R. Carper, University of Maine at Portland-Gorham; William C. Carroll, Boston University; R. L. Caserio, SUNY at Buffalo; David Cavitch, Tufts University; Thomas H. Chalfant, Alabama State University; Seymour Chatman, University of California, Berkeley; John A. Christie, Vassar College; Priscilla P. Clark, University of Illinois, Chicago; Mother Mary Clement, s.h.c.j., Our Lady of Angels College; James L. Clifford, Columbia University; Richard Cody, Amherst College; Arthur N. Collins, SUNY at Albany; David B. Comer III, Georgia

Institute of Technology; Frederick W. Conner, University of Alabama in Birmingham; Albert S. Cook, SUNY at Buffalo; Philip Cooper, Jr., University of Maryland, Baltimore County; Gary Corseri, University of Florida; Sister Anne Courtney, College of Mount St. Vincent; Sister Francis Dolores Covella, College of Mount St. Vincent; Patricia Craddock, Boston University; G. Armour Craig, Amherst College; Charles R. Crow, University of Pittsburgh; A. Dwight Culler, Yale University; John Cunningham, Hollins College; Ruth Cunningham, R.S.C.J., Kenwood Academy

Vinnie-Marie D'Ambrosio, Brooklyn College, CUNY; Donald Davie, Stanford University; Robert A. Day, Queens College, CUNY; Paul De Man, Yale University; Robert J. DeMott, Ohio University; Joanne T. Dempsey, Harvard University; Roger Dickinson-Brown, SUNY at Oswego; Thomas F. Dillingham, Stephens College; Muriel Dollar, Caldwell College; E. Talbot Donaldson, Yale University; Sister Rose Bernard Donna, C.S.J., College of Saint Rose; James Downey, Carleton University; Victor Doyno, SUNY at Buffalo; Margaret Duggan, Columbia University; Georgia Dunbar, Manhattan Community College, CUNY; Wayne E. Dunlop, Eastern Nazarene College; Michael Dunne, Middle Tennessee State University

Dwight Eddins, University of Alabama; Doris L. Eder, University of Rochester; Thomas R. Edwards, Rutgers University; Irvin Ehrenpreis, University of Virginia; Ronald B. Ein, Clarkson College of Technology; Scott Elledge, Cornell University; W. R. Elton, Graduate Center, CUNY; Martha W. England, Queens College, CUNY; David V. Erdman, SUNY at Stony Brook and New York Public Library; Sister Marie Eugénie, I.H.M. Immaculata College; Gwynne B. Evans, Harvard University

Charles Fanning, Bridgewater State College; Arthur Fenner, University of Detroit; Alfred R. Ferguson, University of Massachusetts at Boston; Frances C. Ferguson, New Haven, Connecticut; David Ferry, Wellesley College; Anne Fessenden, Amherst College; Stanley E. Fish, University of California, Berkeley; Philip

Fisher, Brandeis University; Avrom Fleishman, Johns Hopkins University; Angus Fletcher, SUNY at Buffalo; Edward G. Fletcher, University of Texas; Dean Flower, Smith College; Robert Folkenflik, University of Rochester; George H. Ford, University of Rochester; Leslie D. Foster, Northern Michigan University; Roger Fowler, Brown University; Richard L. Francis, Western Washington State College; Sloane Frazier, New York, New York; Albert B. Friedman, Claremont Graduate School; Norman Friedman, Queens College, CUNY; Wilbur M. Frohock, Harvard University; William Frost, University of California, Santa Barbara; Northrop Frye, Massey College, University of Toronto

Burdett H. Gardner, Monmouth College; Harry R. Garvin, Bucknell University; Marilyn Gaull, Temple University; Blanche H. Gelfant, Dartmouth College; Walker Gibson, University of Massachusetts; H. K. Girling, York University; Michael Goldman, Queens College, CUNY; George Goodin, Southern Illinois University; A. C. Goodson, SUNY at Buffalo; Gerald T. Gordon, University of Maine; Sister Mary Eugene Gotimer, College of Mount St. Vincent; Terry H. Grabar, Fitchburg State College; Donald Greene, University of Southern California; M. E. Grenander, SUNY at Albany; Robert Griffin, Southern Illinois University at Carbondale; Harvey Gross, University of California, Irvine; Allen Guttmann, Amherst College

Margaret R. Hale, University of Connecticut; Mary Louise Hall, o.p., Siena Heights College; Richard E. Hansen, Mary Washington College; Alfred B. Harbage, Harvard University; Victor Harris, Brandeis University; Phillip Harth, University of Wisconsin; Geoffrey Hartman, Yale University; Joan E. Hartman, Staten Island Community College, CUNY; Richard Haven, University of Massachusetts; Miriam M. Heffernan, Brooklyn College; David Herreshoff, Wayne State University; Elizabeth K. Hewitt, SUNY at Binghamton; Mary Hiatt, Baruch College, CUNY; James L. Hill, Michigan State University; Rev. William B. Hill, s.j., University of Scranton; E. D. Hirsch, Jr., University of Virginia;

Eleanor Hoag, Hampton Institute; C. Fenno Hoffman, Jr., Rhode Island School of Design; Daniel Hoffman, University of Pennsylvania; Laurence B. Holland, Johns Hopkins University; Norman N. Holland, SUNY at Buffalo; Robert M. Holland, Drexel University; Frank S. Hook, Lehigh University; Andrew G. Hoover, Oberlin College; Vivian C. Hopkins, SUNY at Albany; Susan R. Horton, University of Massachusetts at Boston; Richard Howard, New York, New York; Thomas Howard, Gordon College; Elizabeth Huberman, Newark State College; Clayton E. Hudnall, University of Hartford; David A. Huisman, Grand Valley State College; Eleanor N. Hutchens, University of Alabama in Huntsville; Samuel Hynes, Northwestern University

Helen Irvin, Transylvania College; Edward E. Irwin, Austin Peay State University; Joseph J. Irwin, Albion College

Barry D. Jacobs, Montclair State College; Nora C. Jaffa, Smith College; Stanley L. Jedynak, Siena College

Marjorie Kaufman, Mount Holyoke College; Carol Kay, Harvard University; H. T. Keenan, Georgia State University; Walter B. Kelly, Mary Washington College; William H. J. Kennedy, Queensborough Community College, CUNY; Hugh Kenner, University of California, Santa Barbara; Frank Kermode, University College, London; R. Brandon Kershner, University of Florida; Hugh P. Kierans, York University; Galway Kinnell, New York, New York; Karl Kiralis, California State College; Rudolf Kirk, Rutgers University; Meredith M. Klaus, Eastern Michigan University; H. L. Kleinfield, C. W. Post College; Edgar H. Knapp, Pennsylvania State University; Mary E. Knapp, Albertus Magnus College; Christian Koontz, R.S.M., Mercyhurst College; Paul J. Korshin, University of Pennsylvania; Elaine Kramer, Brooklyn College, CUNY; Maurice Kramer, Brooklyn College, CUNY; Frank A. Krutzke, Colorado College

J. Craig La Drière, Harvard University; Mary M. Lago, University of Missouri; Robert Langbaum, University of Virginia; Lewis

Leary, University of North Carolina; Richard Lehan, University
of California, Los Angeles; James Leheny, University of Massachusetts; Herbert Leibowitz, Richmond College, CUNY, Samuel
R. Levin, Graduate Center, CUNY; Philip Levine, Tulane University; M. M. Liberman, Grinnell College; Ely M. Liebow, North-
eastern Illinois University; Paul R. Lilly, Jr., SUNY at Oneonta;
Dwight N. Lindley, Hamilton College; Lawrence Lipking, Princeton University; A. Walton Litz, Princeton University; George
Lord, Yale University; Joseph P. Lovering, Canisius College; Irma
S. Lustig, Broomall, Pennsylvania; Bridget G. Lyons, Rutgers University; Robert Lyons, Queens College, CUNY

Elizabeth MacAndrew, Cleveland State University; Isabel G. Mac-
Caffrey, Harvard University; Muriel H. McClanahan, George
Washington University; E. Allen McCormick, Graduate Center,
CUNY; Marjorie W. McCune, Susquehanna University; Lucy
McDiarmid, Boston University; Stuart Y. McDougal, University
of Michigan; Thomas McFarland, CUNY; Rebecca J. MacIntyre,
Centennial H.S.; Warren J. MacIsaac, Catholic University; Ter-
ence McKenzie, U.S. Coast Guard Academy; Elizabeth T.
McLaughlin, Bucknell University; Donald A. McQuade, Queens
College, CUNY; Sister C. E. Maguire, Newton College; John B.
Mahon, U.S. Coast Guard Academy; C. F. Main, Rutgers Univer-
sity; Alice S. Mandanis, Marymount College of Virginia; Daniel
Marder, University of Tulsa; Paul L. Mariani, University of Mas-
sachusetts; Donald G. Marshall, University of California, Los An-
geles; Wallace Martin, University of Toledo; Mary G. Mason,
Emmanuel College; John K. Mathison, University of Wyoming;
Lloyd W. Mauldin, Columbia Union College; Donald C. Mell, Jr.,
University of Delaware; Sydney Mendel, Dalhousie University;
Lore Metzger, Emory University; John H. Middendorf, Columbia
University; B. Joyce Miller, Bloomsburg State College; J. Hillis
Miller, Yale University; Sister Jeanne P. Mittnight, c.s.j., College
of Saint Rose; Barbara Morehead, Thiel College; Ruth Mortimer,
Library of Harvard University; Sidney P. Moss, Southern Illinois
University at Carbondale; Robert D. Moynihan, SUNY at Oneonta;
W. T. Moynihan, University of Connecticut; Francis Murphy,
Smith College

Rae Ann Nager, Harvard University; Lowry Nelson, Jr., Yale University; Margaret Neussendorfer, Yale University; Donald Noble, University of Alabama; Rev. William T. Noon, s.j., Le Moyne College; Lawrence Noriega, Sweet Briar College

Frank V. Occhiogrosso, Drew University; John S. O'Connor, Charlottesville, Virginia; Agnes M. O'Donnell, Lebanon Valley College; Richard Ohmann, Wesleyan University; James M. Osborn, Yale University; Charles A. Owen, University of Connecticut

Enoch D. Padolsky, Carleton University; Felix L. Paul, West Virginia State College; Ronald Paulson, Johns Hopkins University; Richard Pearce, Wheaton College; Roy H. Pearce, University of California, San Diego; Norman H. Pearson, Yale University; Marjorie G. Perloff, University of Maryland; Leland D. Peterson, Old Dominion University; Henry H. Peyton III, Memphis State University; Barry Phillips, Wellesley College; William Phillips, Rutgers University; Priscilla Piche, Siena Heights College; Paul Pickrel, Smith College; Burton Pike, Queens College, CUNY; Nicholas S. Poburko, Dalhousie University; Joel Porte, Harvard University; William C. Pratt, Miami University; Michael Pressler, University of Connecticut; Robert O. Preyer, Brandeis University; John W. Price, Dartmouth College; Alison H. Prindle, Otterbein College; Dennis J. Prindle, Ohio Wesleyan University; William H. Pritchard, Amherst College; Rosentene B. Purnell, Fisk University

Joseph A. Quinn, University of Windsor; Ricardo J. Quinones, Claremont Men's College

Ralph W. Rader, University of California, Berkeley; James Raimes, Oxford University Press; C. Earl Ramsey, Bryn Mawr College; Helen Randall, Smith College; Joan Reardon, Barat College; David R. Rebmann, University of Florida; Robert Reid, University of Connecticut; John E. Reilly, College of the Holy Cross; Donald H. Reiman, The Carl H. Pforzheimer Library; Jerald Reneau, Cambridge, Massachusetts; Louis A. Renza, Dartmouth College; Emma S. Richards, Kutztown State College; Keith N. Richwine, Western Maryland College; James Rieger, University of Rochester; John C. Riely, Yale University; John R. Roberts, University of Missouri; Leo Rockas, University of Hartford; Caroline C. Rodney, Grand Valley State College; Francis X. Roellinger, Oberlin College; Phillip W. Rogers, Queen's University; Kenneth Rosen, University of Maine at Portland-Gorham; Sergio Rossi, University of Padua; Hans H. Rudnick, Southern Illinois University at Carbondale; Rebecca D. Ruggles, Brooklyn College, CUNY; Sister M. Paton Ryan, r.s.m., Marquette University; Robert C. Ryan, Boston University

Phillips Salman, Cleveland State University; Thomas N. Salter, Eastern Connecticut State College; Dorothy I. J. Samuel, Tennessee State University; Arthrell D. Sanders, North Carolina Central University; James L. Sanderson, Rutgers University; Stephen Schmidt, Brandeis University; Helene M. Schnabel, New York, New York; Elisabeth Schneider, Temple University; Robert Scholes, Brown University; Ronald Schuchard, Emory University; H. T. Schultz, Dartmouth College; Richard J. Sexton, Fordham University; Per Seyersted, Oslo University; Marc Shell, Yale University; Heather B. Shih, University of Maryland; William H. Sievert, Pace College; Norman Silverstein, Queens College, CUNY; Calvin Skaggs, Drew University; Sister Mary Francis Slattery, George Washington University; Janet Slemon, Harvard University; Carol H. Smith, Rutgers University; Marcel Smith, University of Alabama; Paul Smith, Trinity College; Susan Snyder, Swathmore College; Ian Sowton, York University; Mark Spilka, Brown University; Robert Spiller, University of Pennsylvania; Thomas F. Staley, University of Tulsa; Susan Staves, Brandeis University; John Stedmond, Queen's University; Edna L. Steeves, University of Rhode Island; A. Wilbur Stevens, Prescott College; Holly Stevens, Yale University; Garrett Stewart, Boston University; Keith Stewart, University of Cincinnati; Donald R. Stoddard, Skidmore College; Albert Stone, Jr., Hellenic College; Albert E. Stone, Emory University; Rudolf F. Storch, Tufts University; Mark Strand, Brooklyn College, CUNY; Jean Sudrann, Mount Holyoke College; Maureen Sullivan, University of Pennsylvania; William P. Sullivan, Marshall University; Stanley Sultan, Clark University; Joseph H. Summers, University of Rochester; U. T. Miller Summers, Rochester Institute of Technology; John Sutherland, Colby College; Donald R. Swanson, Wright State University

Marian C. Tarbox, Winchester, Massachusetts; Edward W. Tayler, Columbia University; Thomas J. Taylor, University of Virginia; Elizabeth Tenenbaum, Vassar College; Robert D. Thornton, State University College; Nancy M. Tischler, Pennsylvania State University, Capitol Campus; Tzvetan Todorov, Centre National de la Recherche Scientifique; David O. Tomlinson, U.S. Naval Academy; Margret G. Trotter, Agnes Scott College; Hoyt Trowbridge, University of New Mexico; Anne Troy, Grand Valley State College

Virginia W. Valentine, University of South Florida, Tampa; R. T. Van Arsdel, University of Puget Sound; Kent T. van den Berg, Yale University; Sara van den Berg, Fairfield University; Charles Vandersee, University of Virginia; Sharon Vanhall, Grand Valley State College; Helen Vendler, Boston University; Howard P. Vincent, Kent State University; Victor E. Vogt, Wesleyan University

Eugene M. Waith, Yale University; Joseph J. Waldmeir, Michigan State University; Emily M. Wallace, Philadelphia, Pennsylvania; Aileen Ward, Brandeis University; Elizabeth G. Warner, Boston University; Janet Warner, York University; Earl R. Wasserman, Johns Hopkins University; Judy Weil, University of Connecticut; Sister Mary Anthony Weinig, Rosemont College; Philip M. Weinstein, Swarthmore College; Edward R. Weismiller, George Washington University; J. K. Welcher, C. W. Post College; Ronald A. Wells, U.S. Coast Guard Academy; Donald Wesling, University of California, San Diego; Barry Westburg, University of Rochester; Faith Westburg, Carleton University; James H. Wheatley, Trinity College; Sister Elizabeth White, Newton College; Robert O. White, Dorchester, Massachusetts; George A. Whiteside, Jr., Rutgers University; Ruth Whitman, Radcliffe College;

Maurita Willett, University of Illinois; Louisa W. G. Williams, John C. Calhoun Junior College; Dorothy Willis, Woodbridge, Connecticut; Elkin C. Wilson, New York University; Mrs. Elkin C. Wilson, Birmingham, Alabama; John H. Wilson, Holy Cross College; Kenneth J. Wilson, University of Rochester; James I. Wimsatt, University of North Carolina at Greensboro; Mary Ann Wimsatt, Greensboro College; W. K. Wimsatt, Yale University; Thomas G. Winner, Brown University; William R. Wolfe, Middle Tennessee State University; Mr. and Mrs. Morris H. Wolff, Temple University; Thomas F. Woods, Grand Valley State College; Samuel K. Workman, Newark College of Engineering; Mildred Worthington, Bentley College; H. Bunker Wright, Miami University (Ohio)

Ruth Yeazell, Boston University; Donald L. Young, Eastern Nazarene College; James D. Young, Georgia Institute of Technology

Paul G. Zomberg, Grand Valley State College